THIS BOOK WAS GIVEN TO

ABBY TESTANI

by

Lissa Williams

on

5/11/2021

If
YOU KNOW WHO
YOU ARE
—
YOU WILL KNOW
WHAT
TO DO

For Abby,
Congratulations on your
graduation! Ron Greer
May 2021

"Ron Greer's wise counsel has helped thousands of persons find health and wholeness in their lives. Many of us are all-too-familiar with the destructive power of hypocrisy. However, Ron expertly offers a framework for living life well—a life of personal and moral integrity. I wholeheartedly recommend this book to anyone who wants to experience God's grace amidst the complexities of life."

—**Bill Britt**, Senior Minister, Peachtree Road United Methodist Church

---

"Ron Greer's *If You Know Who You Are... You'll Know What to Do* is a thoughtful and inspiring examination of a core value—integrity—that cries for attention in a fragile world feeding on uncertainty and conflict. Greer's personal commitment to the Christian ethic shines through his words, not as battering, in-your-face sermonizing, but as reasoning well-measured and sensible. To me, the book is a reminder of the potential of mankind, rather than a condemnation of the failures we all know too well."

—**Terry Kay**, author of *To Dance with the White Dog* and *The Book of Marie*

If
YOU KNOW WHO
YOU ARE

—

YOU WILL KNOW
WHAT
TO DO

LIVING *with* INTEGRITY

———————————

RONALD J. GREER

Abingdon Press / *Nashville*

IF YOU KNOW WHO YOU ARE...
YOU WILL KNOW WHAT TO DO:
LIVING *with* INTEGRITY

Copyright © 2009, 2012 by Abingdon Press
All rights reserved.

2019 Paperback edition with discussion questions ISBN: 978-1-5018-9871-6

2012 Hardcover edition with discussion questions ISBN: 978-1-4267-4461-7

Original Paperback edition published in 2009 as ISBN: 978-0-687-65773-5

The Library of Congress has cataloged the original paperback edition as follows:

Greer, Ronald J., 1947–
    If you know who you are—you'll know what to do : living with integrity / Ronald
J. Greer.
        p.   cm.
    Includes bibliographical references.
    ISBN 978-0-687-65773-5 (pbk. : alk. paper)
1. Integrity—Religious aspects—Christianity.   I. Title.
    BV4647.I55G74   2009
2418.4—dc22

                                                    2009006164

All scripture quotations, unless noted otherwise, are taken from the New Revised Standard Version of the Bible, copyright 1989, Division of Christian Education of the National Council of the Churches of Christ in the United States of America. Used by permission. All rights reserved.

Scripture quotations marked RSV are taken from the Revised Standard Version of the Bible, copyright 1952 [2nd edition, 1971] by the Division of Christian Education of the National Council of the Churches of Christ in the United States of America. Used by permission. All rights reserved.

Scripture quotations marked ASV are taken from the American Standard Version of the Bible.

19 20 21 22 23 24 25 26 27 28—10 9 8 7 6 5 4 3 2 1
MANUFACTURED IN THE UNITED STATES OF AMERICA

To those I have been honored
to know who have lived their lives
with integrity, character, and grace

CONTENTS

Contents

By my integrity I am defined. Out of that integrity I make the choices that become my life.

A friend was sitting at a conference table with colleagues at his company. He was struggling to be understood. Their legal counsel was explaining the nuances of what was technically within the letter of the law. Finally my friend, somewhat exasperated, said, "I'm not asking if it's legal. I'm asking if it's right."

Integrity ... it's doing the right thing when we know it's the right thing to do. It's who we are. It's being true to the lives to which we have been called. It's who we are when someone's watching and when there is not a soul in sight.

It's called *integrity*.

Integrity is vital throughout life. Our circumstances change.

We grow and mature. We are always searching for what makes us whole, for what we believe, for who we are at our finest in each of life's challenges and joys.

This book is an appeal for personal integrity, and it is a call for moral integrity. *Personal* integrity is when we are authentically the persons we were created to be. It means living a life of wholeness and congruence. *Moral* integrity is when we do what is right simply because we know it is the right thing to do. It means living a life of character and virtue. Integrity takes both.

I have written this book in the only way I know to write: as though I am speaking to you, just as I would to a friend about something that is important. My goal is to help in the discovery of what it means to live as God created us, congruent with the life to which we are called.

In this writing I tell stories. Some come from my life, while most are drawn from the lives of others. You might think of these stories as metaphors. I think of them as parables.

Parable is an interesting word. Culturally, it has been shaped to mean "a story with a lesson," but that is so much less than what the word originally meant. *Parable* meant "a placing beside," from the Greek *parabole*, meaning "to compare." A parable is something placed alongside something else to compare, to illuminate, and to understand it more clearly.[1]

Jesus' stories were parables—stories he placed alongside the stories of our lives to illuminate them, to convey a meaning and depth we might never have seen before. Think of the stories in this book that way—stories meant for you to place beside your story, to see if it turns on any new lights or resonates with your life, your integrity.

> *An elderly man once spoke out of the wisdom gained from a lifetime of rich experience. "As I have aged, my priorities have changed and narrowed. I am down to one. I focus on it daily, and my life is guided by it. It is, 'Don't fall.'"*

Like that elderly man, my priorities have changed as well. The longer I live, the more I, too, focus on the fundamentals. "Don't fall": don't fall away from the person God created me to be. I focus on this principle daily, and my life is guided by it.

By my integrity I am defined. Out of that integrity I make the choices that become my life.

PART I

PERSONAL INTEGRITY:
A LIFE OF WHOLENESS

"Is not . . . the integrity of your ways your hope?"
Job 4:6

The story is told about Hendrik Kraemer, a remark-able lay missionary from the Dutch church who spent much of his adult life in Indonesia. He was in his native Holland when the Second World War broke out. The Gestapo dominated the nation of Holland, forcing Dutch Jews to places like Buchenwald and Dachau.

Late one night a group of Dutch laypersons came to see Hendrik Kraemer. They said to him, "Dr. Kraemer, what shall we do? Our neighbors are dying. We don't know what is going to become of us as a nation. Please, please, if you can, tell us what to do. We have got to do something, and we have got to do it now."

And Hendrik Kraemer said to them, "I am not going to tell you what to do, but I will tell you who you are. And

if you know who you are, then you will know what to do."
He opened his Bible to 1 Peter and began to read:

"You are a chosen race, a royal priesthood, a dedicated nation, and a people claimed by God as his own, to proclaim the triumphs of Him who has called you out of darkness and into his marvelous light."

Dr. Kraemer closed his Bible. "Do you know who you are?" he asked, "Then you'll know what to do." Thanking him, the group left his house. That night, they formed the Dutch Resistance.

I heard this account decades ago, and through all these years Hendrik Kraemer's statement to that group remains a powerful anchor in my life.

"If you know who you are, you will know what to do."

When faced with a difficult decision, when presented with an awkward dilemma, I have remembered.

In moments I seek to be grounded as the person I am, I remember.

When I seek to be anchored as the person God created me to be, I remember.

I remember it as I seek to live with integrity. I remember it when confusions, shallowness, expediency, and self-centeredness are pulling me away from what has character, what has authenticity, and what is right for me.

As a pastoral counselor, most of the people I see bring specific problems or issues with which they want to deal. We spend the time required to address them. And then, they may say, there is something more they need—something less specific, less well-defined, but equally important.

Life is good, but... Something isn't quite in place. Something isn't connecting. Something seems to be missing. In countless ways they may have it all. *All,* that is, except fulfillment, meaning, and joy. How empty it is to awaken without a purpose to the day. These people have lost touch with something precious. They have lost touch with their depths, their wholeness, their congruence, their souls—with the person God created when God created each of them in their own uniqueness.

They have lost their *integrity,* the very thing that keeps them together as a whole human being. They haven't lost their way so much as they have lost touch with the person they are. Over the years I have come to see integrity for what it is—essential. It is required for anyone seeking to live, as Jesus put it, a*bundantly.*

It is reported that Pablo Casals once had a young cellist play for him to get feedback from the master. When the young cellist had finished, Casals's critique was spoken in a single sentence: "You hit all the right notes, but you didn't play the music."

This lack of integrity can be found in some of the finest people. They hit all the right notes. They live moral lives with charity and compassion. Yet they are empty and are seeking purpose. It isn't quite depression they feel. It's more like something is missing, something important isn't aligned. They lack focus and direction. They don't feel complete or whole. Integrity is missing.

So, what is *integrity*? The major dictionaries are similar in their understandings. *The American Heritage Dictionary* describes integrity as

The state of being unimpaired; soundness.

The quality or condition of being whole or undivided; completeness.

Steadfast adherence to a strict moral or ethical code.[1]

Two important understandings of the word emerge. First, *integrity* means wholeness. It involves living in harmony with myself—where my thinking and my feeling and my acting are in sync. This is when what I believe, and how I feel and the way I live are congruent.

Integrity comes from the Latin *integer,* meaning whole, integrated, complete. It is where my beliefs, convictions, thoughts, and behaviors are integrated together into my life. This first meaning of the term was in use before A.D. 1400.[2]

Then by the mid-sixteenth century a second understanding of integrity merged with this idea of wholeness, involving values such as honesty. The person of integrity intentionally follows a moral or ethical code. A major element in my completeness as a person is following the set of values in which I believe and by which I strive to live.

As Yale professor Stephen Carter put it, "Integrity, applied to a person, carries more than a sense of wholeness, because a person must have something to be whole about."[3] Moral integrity includes those convictions and commitments that define who I am, that shape the person I intentionally strive to be.

After Hendrik Kraemer made his profound statement, "If you know who you are, then you will know what to do," he reached for his Bible. Integrity involves both the uniqueness of who I am as a person and the integration of the values and wisdom that guide me.

This first understanding of integrity involves being the person I am. The second involves being the *person of faith* I am.

The former is my personal integrity. The latter is my *moral integrity*.

These two meanings of integrity comprise the two main parts of this book. The first, "Personal Integrity: A Life of Wholeness," focuses on the discernment, the acknowledgment, and the living out of who I am as a person. In this first part, the chapter "Markers of Integrity" establishes the foundation of what *integrity* means and why it is of such importance. The dangers and pitfalls of disconnecting from our authenticity are addressed in the following two chapters, "Wandering Off Your Path" and "Three Detours." The final chapter in this section, "Who Am I *Now*?" reminds us that lives of integrity are lives in process: though my core identity may remain largely unchanged, it will need to respond to new calls and be applied to new situations.

The second part of this book, "Moral Integrity: A Person of Values," is about the virtues, values, and directions to which I commit myself as a person of faith. We will focus on the values we hold in common and those you personally hold as uniquely important in defining who you are.

CHAPTER ONE

MARKERS
OF INTEGRITY

Whoever walks in integrity walks securely.
—Proverbs 10:9

I grew up with a simple view of integrity. It involved a kind of Boy Scout, well-scrubbed notion of doing the right thing and not telling a lie. It was a start.

Integrity is much more than *not telling a lie*—it's not lying to myself. It's more than telling the truth—it's being true to who I am. To be a person of integrity is to strive to be true to the person I was created to be. It is to strive to be that person consistently across the whole of my life—in my spiritual life, in my marriage, in my family, in my vocation, in picking up the laundry, in buying the groceries, in playing a round of golf. It is to be who God formed me to be at my finest and most authentic.

If you know who you are, you'll know what to do.

Integrity involves wholeness and authenticity. It is living a life consistent with who I am within. It is living a life that requires my thoughts, my feelings, and my actions to be congruent, to be the union of who I am within—what I believe, who I understand myself to be, and how I live my life. Integrity gives rise to the clichés of "getting it together" and "having it all together."[4] This understanding of integrity is in the same spirit as Mahatma Gandhi's words, "Happiness is when what you think, what you say, and what you do are in harmony."

Integrity involves taking the personality that is mine from birth and integrating the values, virtues, and wisdom with which I identify and have come to claim. It always involves *character*, referred to in my dictionary as "moral excellence." I love that.

Integrity is a word with universal appeal. It is used in a variety of professions and arenas—yet always with that same understanding of wholeness and fidelity to principle.

At the other extreme of the idea of *integrity* is a word Jesus used so scathingly: *hypocrisy*. It comes from the Greek word hupokrites, once used to refer to actors—those who are pretending to be what they are not—those who are divided from their true selves.[5]

Integrity means "whole, complete." *Hypocrisy* means "divided, acting." Hypocrisy is pretending to be something in my heart and soul that I am not.

Here's what's spooky: the actor often doesn't know he's acting. *No, we don't, do we?* The actor may be living out his social role, doing it the way it's always been done, the way he was taught—never engaging in his own discernment, never hearing his soul's voice, the call of God, the yearning of his own integrity.

He may be living a fine, upstanding life, making a significant contribution to his community, but the renewing vitality that comes from tapping into the wellspring of his soul is absent. He has a winsome smile, a hearty handshake, but as an actor living out a role, albeit unaware, much of his life's potential is left on the table. I won't quite say that the unexamined life is not worth living, but I will say the unexamined life is lessened and diminished in worth.

I have always loved how the church I attend encourages each of us to stay alive spiritually and theologically. We are challenged to think for ourselves. This church does not slam a theological stance down our throats. It encourages us to think, to discern, and to discover who God is in each of our lives. I suppose it might be easier if someone were to tell me who God is in my life, but it would have so much less meaning—and, without the struggle of discernment, less integrity.

One way of developing discernment at our church is a program called the DISCIPLE Bible study. This excellent study does not tell us who God is for us, but it helps us discover God in a way that is profoundly personal and meaningful.

I shall always remember the phone call received by an assistant pastor teaching DISCIPLE. The call was from a minister of another denomination asking about the study and requesting some materials on it. The pastor was glad to send them. A few days later the minister phoned again. He was extremely complimentary about the quality of the study, saying that the materials were beautifully presented and that the questions in each section were so clear and on point. There was only one problem, he said: "You forgot to send me the answer book."

The answer book to many of life's most vital questions can be found only on the journey to the depth of one's own heart and soul.

I think of the parable of the younger son who left his father and his home with his inheritance (see Luke 15:11-32). It's as familiar as parables get. Perhaps it's familiar not just because we've *heard* it so often, but because we've *lived it* so often.

With fresh eyes, let's look at him, this "prodigal son" as he often is called, and let's agree not to be too tough on him. He simply wanted to experience life. Did he intend to crash and burn? Of course not. Just like the rest of us, he was a kid trying to grow up—experiencing life, trying things out, discovering who he was. And in so doing, he made some mistakes; some were serious mistakes. He went for what felt good, what he thought would make him happy.

In trying to *discover* who he was, he became *disconnected* from what he was. Through a brilliant use of irony and humor, to show how truly disconnected this fine Jewish boy had become, Jesus puts him in a field feeding pigs—hardly a rung on his intended vocational career ladder.

I've certainly been there. Fortunately, no pigs were involved. I began with the best of intentions, launching into some new venture only to discover that it wasn't me. It may have been a fine path for someone else, but not for me. I didn't fit. I didn't belong. It didn't have integrity—*for me.*

So there this young man in the parable sat, perhaps on a fence, overlooking a field of pigs, staring down at a handful of corn he was about to throw—about as lost a soul as you will ever find, about as disconnected from himself as anyone you will ever see. And there, Jesus said, he "came to himself" (verse 17). Suddenly it wasn't corn the young man was seeing; it was a mirror. He looked into his heart of hearts and remembered who he was.

He *came to himself.* He went from being divided to being connected. It was a moment of integrity. He got up, dropped the corn on the ground, and walked straight into the life he had been created to live.

If you know who you are, you'll know what to do.

This younger son is going to have to share some room on that fence with each of us from time to time. Sometimes we get lost. Sometimes badly. We forget who God created us to be. Sometimes not *so* badly. It just feels like we have missed a turn.

Into my office walks a middle-aged woman. A wonderful person in so many ways, but if you look carefully into her eyes you can see her emptiness. How does that saying go? The lights are on, but nobody's home. It's called depression. She started out with so many dreams and so much hope . . . but something happened.

Maybe she got too caught up in letting society define her, or perhaps her husband leaned on her and pressured her to be who he wanted her to be. Somehow her spirit broke or her priorities shifted, and she has found herself sitting on that same fence alongside the prodigal, wondering what happened, wondering where she went awry.

The fellow on the fence went awry looking for a shortcut to *feeling good*. Often that's the wrong turn we all make. The question in faithful living isn't "Does it feel good?" but "Does it feel right?" Now, those times when what feels good is the same thing as what feels right, we've got it made. But when they are two distinct choices and we've got to choose one or the other, then integrity says to go with what feels right. Paul could not have put it more clearly: "Do not be weary in doing what is right" (2 Thessalonians 3:13). When you are faced with such choices, you have to ask yourself, *Does it have integrity? Is it based on a life lived with character?*

Jesus underscores the importance of this young man's self-discovery, as he has the father saying to his other son, "This brother of yours was dead and has come to life; he was lost and has been found" (Luke 15:32). So much of life and its vitality and meaning are *dead* when that precious connection with heart and soul is lost.

So integrity means my life is whole and is congruent. But what is involved in achieving that authenticity? Clearly there are no quick-and-easy steps. There is no shortcut. Yet I believe there are some markers each of us will find along the way. There are some tasks required in order to be successful in engaging this journey.

Integrity requires that

I discover who I am.

I claim who I am.

I live who I am.

I DISCOVER WHO I AM

Integrity—living with character—first requires discovering, discerning who you are, asking yourself:

What do I value?
What do I believe?
What is important?
What is precious?
What is sacred to me?

Integrity involves discerning who you are, and then where—and to what—you feel called at this moment in your life. Integrity implies that I have a core, a spiritual center in which I am grounded and from which I live out my life. It often means to pause in the quiet, with everything electronic turned off, to listen, to discern, to "be still, and know" (Psalm 46:10), believing there is a voice of wisdom to be heard.

If you know who you are . . .

I wish issues of integrity involved only choices of right versus wrong. Those are relatively easy. Or at least they are clear. It's when life is lived in the gray—as most of life is—that it gets complicated. The choices are more subtle. The choices are between "right" and what is "right for me." They require reflection, self-knowledge, and prayerful self-examination. I must pause and listen, ready to learn, to receive. Educator and author Parker

Palmer said it well: "Before you tell your life what you intend to do with it, listen for what it intends to do with you."[6]

I was once asked to speak to a group of high-school girls who were mostly older teens, soon to go to college. The topic was sexual ethics. The most important idea I wanted to tell them was, "Know who you are. You alone can discern that. Know who you are before your date rings the doorbell. Don't make it up after a few beers and the hormones are raging. Take the time to get to know you and your values. Listen to your heart and discover what you really believe. Know who you are before you answer the door."

The word *authentic* frequently is used, sometimes almost synonymously, with the word *integrity*. It is interesting that its origin is from the Greek word *authentikos*, which means "one who acts on his *own* authority" (emphasis added).[7] I cannot successfully define myself from outside myself. That definition is between God and me. Those outside me can inform me and even inspire me but never define me. I must discern that role for myself.

I believe this is what Jesus meant when he said, "A man shall leave his father and mother" (Mark 10:7). Men and women, having reached their own adulthood, should no longer be looking outside themselves for authority figures to direct their lives—no longer living out of the expectations of others. They will have moved beyond peer pressure influencing them into some herd mentality. They will have matured and claimed their own sense of authority within as they continually discover who God created them to be and about what God calls them to be.

It's not unusual for a concerned parent to stop me in the hall before church, as this man does. He tells me that over the Thanksgiving break he and his wife have learned that their daughter, a college freshman, has not been to church a single time during her entire first semester.

I ask him, "Okay, Bob, now what's your problem?"
"My problem is she hasn't been to a single church—Methodist, Baptist, Presbyterian, or otherwise." With a slight smile I say to my friend, "I understand that, but what's your problem?" About that time he says, "I thought you were a minister!"

I reply, "I am, Bob, and you don't have a problem. She's a freshman in college. She's not 'supposed' to go to church. (I think it's in the unofficial college student's handbook somewhere.) But don't worry. I know Susie, and she'll be back. It may be next month or next year or after she gets married or has her baby baptized. But she'll be back. And when she does, there will be an important difference. She'll be coming to church not as a girl who is supposed to, but as a woman who chooses to."

The apostle Paul wrote, "When I became an adult, I put an end to childish ways" (1 Corinthians 13:11). I am who I am as an adult because that is who I have discovered myself to be, feel called to be, and have chosen to be.

Sometimes that discovery is easy. It slaps us in the face with its clarity. Other times, God is so frustrating with that "still small voice" (1 Kings 19:12 RSV).

Discernment: that's our first task.

I CLAIM WHO I AM

Having engaged in this discovery of who I am, I must then intentionally claim what I have discovered to be important, precious, and sacred for my life. These are the values I choose to be "about" in my life. It is one thing to *know* them; it is another thing to commit myself to them. If I am to live with integrity, I must choose to be defined by what I believe to be true for me.

Many values I hold are those I was taught, those shared by my community. Yet the fact that they are deemed by those whom I respect to be worthy and important simply isn't enough. These values had to become *my* values. They are mine only when I claim them as *mine*. Lynne McFall puts it well: "One must speak 'in the first person,' (to) make one's principles, conventional or otherwise, one's own."[8]

I must make clear, conscious choices in defining who I am. Often we hear of the debate between nature and nurture, the question of which is the most important determinant in who we become as persons. I have always felt there is a third factor that has been left out of the debate: choice. I am both blessed and limited by my genetic wiring and my upbringing, but then I have great freedom in what I choose to do with these raw materials nature and nurture have given me. That choice is crucial.

Knowing who I am is the key to the first step, but it is not enough. Jesus spoke with those who *knew* who they were called to be, but instead of claiming it, some "went away grieving" (Matthew 19:22). *Knowing* is not enough. I must be intentional in committing to be the person in my heart of hearts I know I am at my deepest and finest. This takes an awareness and makes it into a decision.

I LIVE WHO I AM

Having discerned who I am and having claimed intentionally what I believe to be true for me, it is time for me to act—it's time to give traction to what I have discovered. Stephen Carter says that integrity begins with, first, "*discerning* what is right and what is wrong" and then "*acting* on what you have discerned, even at personal cost."[9]

> *I was sitting in the Atlanta airport, waiting at Gate 32 to board a plane. Zones 1 and 2 were called. I stood, picked up my briefcase, and walked toward the line that was forming. As I passed a row of seats I heard a girl ask her mother, "Do I stand up now?"*
>
> *Something about the girl's voice got my attention. She was developmentally disabled. I kept walking, got in line, and boarded the plane.*

I took my place in seat 7C. After I settled in, I looked up. There was the girl, coming down the aisle by herself. I was surprised to see that she was a teenager—she was so petite that she appeared almost frail. The seat in front of mine was hers.

Then "Animal House" boarded. A group of college students came down the aisle and took several rows of seats across from us. They were laughing, joking with one another, and having a great time. But above all else, they were being cool. Cool, you understand, was imperative.

Finally, the plane was pushed back and began taxiing. Ten minutes later the pilot announced that we were cleared for takeoff. He made the final turn onto the runway.

I looked up and saw that little head with the brunette hair lean partway across the aisle. I heard the girl say to the college student across from her, "I get real nervous when we take off. Would you hold my hand?"

My eyes were riveted on the young man to see what he would do. Holding a stranger's hand is not cool. After an initial nervous blush, he began to smile, and halfway across the aisle came that kid's big ol' hand. The girl's tiny hand grabbed it and squeezed.

There they held hands, across the aisle, as our Delta jet was airborne.

There they held hands as all his friends sat in disbelief. There they held hands as I stared, also in disbelief, and memorized that sacred moment. I knew I was witnessing a sacrament.

The plane's wheels clunked into place beneath us. She let go of his hand and said something to him. The engines were now so loud, I couldn't hear.

For the next hour and a half he read his Harry Potter book. She listened to her iPod.

Then the plane descended as we approached Shreveport. In those few moments, as we anticipated the jolt of the runway, this young man turned to the girl and—as I read his lips—asked, "Do you need to hold my hand?"

Apparently she said, "No." He smiled and nodded.

Having discerned who we are, it is then time to act. It may not be cool for a young man in college to hold hands with a girl who is disabled, but he was responding to a voice within him, the voice of his integrity. Living with integrity requires clarity of purpose, commitment to values, and then courage—the courage to live what we believe even at personal cost.

If you know who you are, you'll know what to do.

When I look back on the regrets of my life, most are not from moments in which I did something wrong or hurtful, but those times when something was called for—some word, some action, some deed—and from within me I heard my soul's voice calling to me to act, *but I did nothing.* Out of my passivity came my hypocrisy: feeling one way and doing the other. Not whole. Divided.

Benjamin Franklin said it beautifully: "As we must account for every idle word, so we must account for every idle silence."

Live with integrity. Live intentionally. Live authentically. Live boldly. Leave nothing on the table; let there be *very* few regrets.

Novelist Elie Wiesel tells the story of a Hasidic rabbi named Zusya. Zusya was a timid man, a man who concealed more than he revealed. One day Zusya stood before his congregation and said, "When I die and have to present myself before the celestial tribunal, they will not ask me, 'Zusya, why were you not Moses?' Because I would say, 'Moses was a prophet, and I am not.'

"They would not say, 'Zusya, why were you not Jeremiah?' For I would say, 'Jeremiah was a writer, and I am not.' And they will not say, 'Why were you not Rabbi Akiba?' For I would tell them, 'Rabbi Akiba was a great teacher, and I am not.'

"But then they will say, 'Zusya, why were you not Zusya?' And to this, I will have no answer."[10]

CHAPTER TWO

WANDERING OFF YOUR PATH

Do not be conformed to this world, but be transformed by the renewing
of your minds, so that you may discern what is the will of God—what is
good and acceptable and perfect.
—Romans 12:2

Our daughter Brooke was a young child when the
song "Right Here Waiting," by Richard Marx, was
released. It had a beautiful melody, and for months she
loved singing it.

The theme of the song is actually one of romantic
dependency. Whatever his partner does, or however she
may break his heart, the refrain goes, "I will be right here
waiting for you."

One day Brooke was riding in the car with her mother, singing along with the words. Brooke's singing got softer and softer, until she stopped altogether. She was now staring at the radio, taking in the words for the first time. She listened carefully to this chorus celebrating unhealthy dependency. Then, talking directly into the radio, she all but shouted, "Get a life!"

We can all identify with the writer of the song. It is tempting to want to look outside ourselves to find what will make us whole. It is tempting to want to find someone else to complete us, or to adapt to some role to define us. It is tempting, as shortcuts usually are. But it leaves us cut off from the lives that we have discerned *will* make us whole—lives that only we can define. It leaves us estranged from the God who invites us to that authenticity.

We wander. We sometimes wander off course. No matter how important integrity may be to us, we lose our way. We find ourselves living in disharmony. The lives we are living are no longer fitting with who we are. In this chapter, and the next, we focus on those awkward, difficult times of incongruence.

Joseph Campbell has said that to be who you are is the privilege of life. The *calling* of life is, also, to be who you are.

It sounds good, but it's not so easy. In fact, it can be really tough. We live with conflicting purposes and mixed motives. The apostle Paul likely said it best: "I do not understand my own actions. For I do not do what I want, but I do the very thing I hate" (Romans 7:15). Even after we have discerned, claimed, and chosen to live with the wholeness of our integrity, we slip up. We follow another route. Somehow we take a turn that isn't ours. We move in a direction that isn't a bad one, but it isn't ours. It brings little meaning or fulfillment. And over time it becomes familiar. It becomes our new life. Then something jolts us—some event serves as a mirror for us—and we look around and wonder how in the world we got here.

So what happened? How did we find ourselves in the middle of lives without integrity? What are the reasons we wander off the path?

IGNORING INTEGRITY

At the most fundamental level, the loss of integrity is consciously, intentionally choosing what we know is wrong over what is right. Rocket science is not required to figure out the motivation of this one. It's going with what feels good over what feels right. What feels good may be the avoidance of anxiety or fear or insecurity that would come with the difficult choice. Or the motive may be a shallow, straightforward desire for nothing but pleasure and immediate gratification. I think we could call that unvarnished greed.

The infamous J. R. Ewing, a character on the television show Dallas, said it clearly: "Once you get past integrity, the rest is a piece of cake." A corner is cut, albeit a small one, and the twinge of guilt isn't that bad. He or she has taken the first step onto the moral slippery slope. The next corner that is cut may be a bit more severe, as is the next—until integrity is rarely a consideration. The result is a denial of the self.

At best, this lifestyle is one of superficiality. Those who have gotten past integrity have gotten past making moral and ethical values a priority in decision-making. Their perspective is self-absorbed and self-centered. What is sought is whatever brings the rush, the momentary happiness, the money, the immediate gratification. A life grounded in moral or personal values is sacrificed for the immediate pleasure of the moment.

A politician receives trips and gifts before voting for legislation benefiting his more-than-gracious hosts. Another public servant offers an appointed position to the highest bidder. Athletes take prohibited anabolic steroids to tilt what was supposed to be a level playing field. Business insiders quietly buy or sell their shares just as the company prepares to make its big announcement. A company manufacturing ladders makes a strategic, economic decision to use a cheaper grade of aluminum, calculating the savings in material to be greater than the losses from lawsuits on behalf of those injured or killed.

At the extreme, ignoring integrity points to sociopathy. The sociopath has no conscience; morality is a meaningless word. Whatever gives pleasure and is expedient is all that is sought. There is no hesitation, no twinge of anything resembling guilt. It is not that values are ignored—they no longer even appear on the radar screen as a consideration.

This is the sacrifice of integrity at its crudest and most base level. I shall move on, since I wrote this for you—and few functioning in this way would have picked up this book, much less be reading it.

RATIONALIZING

Where we may struggle with integrity is in the next rung up from living without regard to values and morality. It is for those who haven't "gotten past integrity." It's when we hear that voice from within our soul telling us the path of integrity, but the pull away is too enticing. Yet, as people of character, we can't just thumb our noses at what is right and wrong. After all, we're decent Christian people. So we do our fancy footwork to change the rules to make what we want to do okay.

It's called *rationalizing*—and it's dangerous.

My dictionary defines *rationalize* as to "cause something to seem reasonable" and "to create an excuse or more attractive explanation."[11] Rationalizing overrides our true voice. It disconnects. It *causes something to seem reasonable* because we want it to seem reasonable. This attempt to justify our action involves denial as we create our own *more attractive* reality.

Living in the tension between conflicting attitudes, desires, or beliefs is called "cognitive dissonance." It occurs when we want two mutually exclusive things, when we travel in two different directions at the same time. Often the conflict is between what *feels good* and what *feels right*. We have to come down on one side or the other. When we choose to go with what feels good, rationalizing is usually the vehicle that gets us there. As ethicist John Truslow put it (with tongue firmly planted in cheek), "When other people violate the moral order, they seem to be bad people. When I do it, I've got pretty good reasons."[12]

And we can be so creative! We take advantage of life being lived in the ambiguity of the gray. Some choices may not be *wrong*, but in my heart of hearts I know; I know better. I know I'm "blowing smoke." That particular choice may not be so bad—say, a few extra calories—but I need to be honest with myself as to what I'm doing and why. If we are going to violate a minor rule, we can at least shoot straight with ourselves and not dance through some silly rationalization.

At the heart of rationalizing is selfishness without honesty. I want what I want, and I'm going to find a way of distorting the facts to make it sound all right. *I know this second helping is off my diet, but it's okay because I worked out on the Thursday before last; in fact, I almost broke a sweat.*

Rationalizing, however, can be far more serious. Thomas Jefferson struggled with this compromise of his integrity much of his adult life. The man who wrote "all men are created equal" in the Declaration of Independence was keenly aware of the contradiction within his own life as an owner of slaves. He justified this continued practice as an economic necessity for a farmer and plantation owner. It was a weak rationalization, and Jefferson knew it. You can feel his agony in several of his later writings, but perhaps none more pronounced than in his book *Notes on the State of Virginia*: "I tremble for my country when I reflect that God is just."[13]

Rationalizations can get us pretty lost as we set aside the compass with which we are guided.

A PATH NOT OURS

Yet there is another way by which we are estranged from ourselves. Somehow, we take a path that isn't ours. It is pervasive among those who are good people seeking to live with character and values. This disconnect is usually not a conscious choice. It really isn't anyone's fault. It may be a good direction for someone else—but not for us.

The possibilities for how this disconnect can happen are limitless. Often we are on *wrong* paths for good reasons—we are wanting to try out something new to see if it fits: a fitness routine, a volunteer opportunity, even a different vocation. Perhaps it works, or maybe *it's just not me*, at least at this point in my life. I may try devoting my time to a worthy fund-raising cause but discover that I want to volunteer in a way that is more "hands-on" with those in need. It is a good cause, and I may be glad I tried it—but it just doesn't fit me.

Others get off track in deeper and more lasting ways. Some adapt to a role that becomes their identity. Perhaps out of personal insecurity they need a role in which they can hide. It is then "their" identity. Out of the fear they won't be accepted as they are, they choose to show to others—and then, over time, ultimately to themselves—only limited parts of who they are. As the role becomes their identity, they lose touch, and even awareness, with all that is buried.

These roles can be a vocation or a person's place within the family or community. It's like a creeping kudzu vine in the South that, before you know it, eventually has taken over the yard. For these persons, in their own minds they are so identified with that function, and likely get so much out of it, that *it becomes who they are*. It becomes their "place" in life. I have seen a version of this in those who have had notable achievements earlier in their lives. Those become their "glory days." The pictures on the walls or the trophies on the mantels are of the era that became their lives—and their permanent identities were frozen in time. The sadness is that they lost touch with who they are today. It's not that they got on the wrong path so much as they stopped taking new paths at all.

Another group who wander off from lives true to their identity are *the pleasers*—who usually are working hard to be liked and accepted. They feel it is their job to make sure those around them are happy, so they deny any part of themselves that would bring displeasure or discomfort to anyone else. It is to this point I always felt Jesus was referring when he said, "Woe to you when all speak well of you" (Luke 6:26). When *all* speak well of anyone, then that person is working entirely too hard to be liked or to be pleasing—and is sacrificing personal integrity in the process. Typically, "the pleaser" has been their role in their families of origin. Though it denies who they are—how they feel and what they want out of life—to please others frees them from the anxiety of not having "done their job."

How they really feel about anything gets so buried, they honestly don't know. For example, the question "Where do you want to go for dinner?" is usually answered with a sincere, "Oh, it doesn't matter." In this example, the woman's answer is honest to how she feels, but it isn't true. It *does* matter to her, but her preference is so buried from years of neglect, she doesn't recognize it. The fact that she *does* have preferences shows when her husband suggests a Chinese restaurant, and she says, "Not tonight." "Mexican?" "I don't think so." "Thai?" "Maybe another time…" You get the idea. We all have times of indecision. But for this woman, out of her desire to please others, she has lost touch with her own basic wants and preferences.

Personal integrity is to have one's thinking, feeling, and acting in harmony. Both those living too much to please and those living out a role, instead of living their true lives, have allowed their thinking to override their feelings and dictate their actions. The result is shutting off the authentic voice that leads to wholeness.

We all comply to a degree, of course, with the expectations of society. We want to be gracious. We develop a *social self* that we can pull out when needed. It is our *persona*, or "mask," as the word is literally translated. But as we are being gracious and social, we have not lost touch with who we are.

The danger is for those for whom the lines are blurred between their social self and their authentic self—between what the world expects of them and the persons God created them to be. They don't know where one leaves off and the other picks up. They successfully push the parts of their lives society deems to be unacceptable into the shadows. In the process, something of their heart and soul is lost. The person God created them to be is set aside. The direction to which God calls them is not heard.

Much of the temptation to live out a role goes back to the adage "if they really knew me, they wouldn't like me." It is so powerful, pervasive, and untrue. My own experience, as one who is private and has lived much of his life showing only limited sides, is quite the contrary. The more I open myself and invite others to know who I am, the more I am accepted, valued, and meaningfully connected.

Living with integrity gives life vitality, energy, and joy. It taps into a spiritual and emotional wellspring by which I am filled and fulfilled. I am being who I am, and I am where I am meant to be at this moment in my life. It is a wonderful feeling. As the scriptures put it, "Keep your heart with all vigilance, / for from it flow the springs of life" (Proverbs 4:23).

FROM CHILDHOOD

It is often from childhood that a girl or boy experiences the disconnection from the true self. It may be the result of a parent's heavy hand or a child's personality that is too compliant, wanting too badly to please.

Families typically assign us roles to live out. For many people it is as if they had been born onto a stage and handed a script for their parts. Each was to live out that role in the family play. Improvisation was not permitted. It's like a friend of mine said, "My older sister was the family rebel. My older brother was the free spirit. When I came along, they wanted—and I became—*a good girl.*"

Or it may have been an especially rigid family where all the children are given the same script, and none may vary from it. (This is so vividly described in Pat Conroy's novel *The Great Santini.*) In yet another family the child may be called to live out a parent's unfulfilled dreams, which may or may not have any relevance to the true life direction of that child.

In each of these families the script may be a close match to who the child is—or perhaps not. Perhaps the child is a creative spirit who is forced always to color within the lines. Or maybe the child is private and introverted but finds herself pushed in front of the footlights. We have all heard those parental voices from fathers on the sidelines or mothers backstage, pushing their children to achieve what are perhaps their unfulfilled dreams.

Psychologist Sheldon Kopp writes, "Too often, as children, we are encouraged to try to be something other than ourselves. It is demanded that we assume a character not our own, live out a life story written by another…"[14] He continues, "I must define myself. Asking others to define me, no matter how kind and trustworthy they may be, is to do myself in."[15]

Parenting, it has been said, isn't *shaping* our children nearly so much as helping them discover what shape their lives already have been given. The passage from Jeremiah echoes the same theme: "Before I formed you in the womb I knew you" (1:5). Clearly, values, principles, rights-and-wrongs are to be taught. Yet the pre-existing unique soul and personality of the child is to be respected; it is God-given and to be honored as we help that child grow and mature into the adult he or she was created to be. So we may be assigned a role as to who we are to be, and how we are to relate, in order to give the family balance. Without enough freedom to be ourselves, something important—some essence of who we are—may be lost.

My father bought an 8mm movie camera when I was about eighteen months old. Like any proud parents, mine immediately whipped the camera out of the box to film their two sons. My brother, Ed, who is four years older, and I were in the film, walking across the spillway of our local lake. It was a delightful home movie of this toddler, walking with very bowed legs, and his older brother, walking behind him, mimicking that awkward gait. Here were two happy, free-spirited boys having a great time.

A few years ago my brother put all of our childhood home movies onto a video format. The one with the bowed legs on the spillway was, of course, the first to be seen. Soon after that segment was a fast-forward several months, to the party on our shared birthday—I was two, and Ed was six. Something was different. Something was beginning to change. What happened to that bow-legged kid walking across the spillway, having a ball? Where did that authentic free spirit go?

Wherever it went, it was being replaced with the anxiety of a little two-year-old boy nervously standing beside his birthday cake, wondering what he was supposed to do next. Granted, it was not the most natural of moments. The kid was in the spotlight of this staged event as half the children of our hometown were lined up to be in the home movie. Anyone would have been a little tense. But I knew I was seeing the beginning of a change. I no longer saw the freewheeling kid who could have been trying to sneak a finger full of icing off that cake while no one was looking.

It was a good childhood with much joy and love, but a pattern had begun. He was too focused on what he was "supposed to be doing" and too out of touch with who he was. Something was being lost. Something that would one day need to be reclaimed.

I had begun to look too closely outside myself for the direction of my life. I was looking for more than the appropriate moral and social guidance. I was looking for *how to be me*. I was looking for something *out there* that can only be discovered *within*. I had unknowingly begun to trade integrity for approval.

Father Thomas Keating wrote, "If we want to be anything other than what God has made us to be, we are wasting time. It will not work. The greatest accomplishment in life is to be what we are, which is God's idea of what he wanted us to be when he brought us into being; and no ideas of ours will ever change it. Accepting that gift is accepting God's will for us, and in its acceptance lies the path to growth and ultimate fulfillment."[16]

Thomas Keating is right: all who are taking paths not their own are wasting time. It will not work. Please know that: it will not work. It will never work. And there are as many ways to stray as there are individual life stories. Those who wander from paths that are theirs become disconnected from so much. They are separated from God-given, valued parts of who they are—so much is dismissed into the shadows that is begging to be reclaimed.

Each of us, no matter how far off we have wandered, hears a call to congruence. It is a call to lives of meaning and joy and abundance.

THREE DETOURS

"Do you still persist in your integrity?"
—Job 2:9

The separation caused by our wandering introduces a second word we place in contrast to integrity: *sin*. Sin is not an action. It is an attitude that results in actions. Sin is when I disconnect from God and from my deepest self. Sinful living is being disconnected from who I am and from that for which I was created. One understanding of sin is "to miss the mark."

A life of integrity is quite the opposite. Integrity means to live with congruence—connecting my life, its purpose and direction, with the God of its creation.

Sin is to miss the mark; integrity is to nail it.

When we sin, we are estranged from who we are. We are separated from God and the life to which we believe he calls us. Many of us feel too sophisticated for the word readily to roll off our tongues—but this *is* what we Christians call *sin*.

A colleague once spoke insightfully to ways by which we are separated from our integrity: "Sin is when we think we are less than we are or greater than we are or anything other than who we are." In succinct fashion, here are three of the ways that we separate from God and from our true selves. Essentially, this points to struggles with self-esteem, narcissism, and authentic self-direction. Let's look at each for a moment.

SELF-ESTEEM

"Sin is when we think we are *less than we are ...*"

Self-identity is to know who we are. *Self-esteem* is to value the self we have come to know. Self-esteem that is healthy and positive believes we are good, we are substantial, and we are of value and worth. Positive self-regard brings confidence in our abilities to meet the challenges of life and in our resiliency to bounce back from the difficulties. These lessons are learned from the life experience of meeting challenges and responding to struggles. With that core sense of worth, we are not afraid to enter into relationships and intimately be known by another as the persons we are. As the cliché goes, persons with solid self-esteem are "comfortable in their own skin."

Theologically, to *claim who we are* is to affirm that we all are created in the image of God. Personally, it is to have explored our lives—to have come to know our heart of hearts—and to affirm the core goodness we have discovered. Not perfect, not infallible, but good. It is to have claimed a core set of values to which we are committed and by which we feel grounded.

To live with integrity is to have a self-identity that is accurate and a self-esteem that is positive and confident. Those who struggle with self-esteem—who see themselves as *less than they are*—are often wounded souls who had childhoods without healthy positive mirroring and with—in many cases—too many critical, damaging blows.

A little girl in need of braces laughs with the abandon only a child feels free to laugh. Her callous and inebriated father blurts out, "You have the ugliest smile." For the rest of her life she never smiles without her hand quickly covering her mouth. Damage done. She will always see herself as less than she is.

A young boy brings home his report card with four A's and only one B. Proudly he hands it to his mother. She looks it over. "You've got to work harder in math," is her only reply. The boy's obsessive-compulsive drive for perfection is his way of running from the private fear that he really isn't good enough.

Even in wonderful families, self-esteem can take some serious blows. Every society, every culture has its image of what it considers its *ideal* to be. All are measured by those standards—which tend to be what most of us are not. Whether the criteria are intelligence, beauty, athleticism, wealth, or personality, many young people deem themselves to be *not good enough*. Don't you just shake your head at the incredible superficiality of these criteria with which all have to deal and many have to suffer?

For persons of each gender, to excel athletically can become an all-consuming passion. Self-worth then comes not from who I am but from how well I perform.

I was saddened to read a few years ago of a poll taken of world-class athletes. They were asked, "You are offered a banned performance-enhancing substance that comes with two guarantees: (1) You will not be caught. (2) You will win every competition you enter for the next five years, and then you will die from the side effects of the substance. Would you take it?" Over half of the athletes said yes.[17]

In virtually any life arena there is such a desperate striving for validation. Those who would choose to end their lives for the sake of the achievement feel little intrinsic worth within themselves. The only real meaning is in what they can achieve.

When they do achieve, they receive esteem from others, giving them the illusion of self-esteem. But it's a phantom. Any time our esteem comes from without, it is not anchored. It is like a rug that can be pulled out from under us at any time. Just ask any *former* celebrity who has known fame and has seen it vanish. Real self-esteem is grounded in who I know I am, not in what others think of me or in how well I play any game.

Yet our society is obsessed with values of remarkable superficiality. Take the issue of beauty. Girls learn of its importance from earliest childhood. This is a theme of many popular children's stories. *The Ugly Duckling* has the well-known central character rejected as long as it was ugly, but when it became a beautiful swan it was accepted and affirmed. The question is appropriately asked, what about the ugly ducking that grows up to be an ugly duck?

Or in *Sleeping Beauty,* the message seems to be that if she hadn't been beautiful, she'd still be sacked out, fast asleep. In *Snow White and the Seven Dwarfs* the question was never, "Mirror, mirror on the wall, who has the greatest integrity... or depth... or wisdom?" No, the question was, "Who is the fairest of them all?" The message, it seems, is if you are not pretty enough, you're not good enough.

The pressure is great—to be good enough; to fit in; hopefully, even to excel in one of these relatively shallow ways.

I recall two bumper stickers I have seen. I never think of one without thinking of the other. The first read, "Childhood is brief, but its effects last a lifetime." This can be true. The effects are often deep and permanent. Positively and negatively.

The second bumper sticker, however, brings a different perspective. Let me first set the context in which I saw it. I was coming to a stop at a traffic light on a four-lane street in Atlanta. In the other lane, already stopped, were half a dozen motorcyclists. I pulled up beside them. Make no mistake, these were anything but Hell's Angels. The minimum age—and I'm being generous—was in the late fifties. This was a group of fellow-geezers on their Harleys, having a ball.

The rider on the bike just beside me had covered his helmet with little sayings, like mini bumper stickers. I would have loved it anyway, but I especially did in the setting of hearing these guys laughing and revving their engines. The message that I remember catching my eye read, "It's never too late to have a happy childhood."

Never. It's never too late.

NARCISSISM

"Sin is when we think we are *greater than we are*..."

The term *narcissism* comes from the Greek myth of the youth Narcissus, who fell in love with his own reflection. It implies egotism and self-centeredness from an attitude of self-importance. You likely have heard the line from the narcissistic Hollywood director who was overheard at a party saying, "But enough talk about me—let's talk about you. What did you think of my latest movie?" Out of their self-centeredness, narcissists never stray far from their favorite topic, themselves. They have a special place of prominence in their own minds and believe they should in yours as well.

There are two key words to remember when wanting to understand persons with a narcissistic personality. The first is *grandiosity*. They each have an exaggerated sense of self-importance and specialness. Someone once said, "Too many people in this world are born on third base who think they've hit a triple." In their eyes they are not just unique, they are special. They think they deserve a status above everyone else—"a legend in his own mind," as I once heard it described.

This is the dynamic the prophet Isaiah was describing when he wrote, "Your wisdom and your knowledge / led you astray, and you said in your heart, / 'I am, and there is no one besides me'" (Isaiah 47:10).

The second descriptive word is *entitlement*. Since persons with a narcissistic personality see themselves as special, they believe they are entitled to be treated in accordance with this elevated status. They don't have to play by the same set of rules.

If they happen to be particularly gifted or attractive or

wealthy or a celebrity and the world treats them as if they were special, their distorted sense of self-importance is erroneously confirmed. If they do not stand out and are treated—as most are—as one of the pack, they become confused, feel misunderstood, and are privately frustrated and angry.

Narcissists have lost touch with the genuine souls of the human beings who reside within. This illusion of self-importance is a defense against knowing the self and being known for who they truly are. This defense is usually the result of subconscious insecurity. The results are tragic: their grandiosity keeps them from contact with the essence of God's image placed within them. Their entitlement makes close, loving relationships virtually impossible, as the narcissist has to remain positioned as the one who is a bit more elevated in importance. His needs and wants are consistently to be given preference. As I once heard it said, "The problem with most self-made men is they tend to worship their creator."

They have lost touch with what gives life meaning and grounding. I think of that embarrassing question James and John asked Jesus in the Gospel accounts. The two apostles were attempting to make future seating arrangements on the dais in the Kingdom, and they asked Jesus if one of them could sit on

Jesus' right and the other on his left. Jesus knew he was hearing some serious narcissism long before it had this name.

In his response to James and John, Jesus spoke to what greatness really means: "Whoever wishes to become great among you must be your servant," he said, "and whoever wishes to be first among you must be slave of all" (Mark 10:43).

Greatness, with integrity, has nothing to do with grandiosity or entitlement. It has nothing to do with power or wealth or influence. It has no desire to be thought of as great. It isn't even focused on oneself. Rather, it points to a self-identity grounded in humility and compassion.

DRIFTING

"Sin is when we think we are *anything other than who we are...*"

It may be we don't feel "less than" or "greater than," but simply that we have lost our way. We've drifted. We have listened to voices that aren't for us, or followed directions that just weren't ours.

We are in need of reconnecting. We all are. Regularly. I live much of my life too incongruently. The moments when my thinking, my feeling, and my acting are in harmony tend to be the exception and not the rule. Yet we strive—with a God-given motivation—for that personal authenticity. According to the Merriam-Webster's Dictionary, *integrity* was the word most looked up online in 2005.[18] There is a longing to get it right.

I once heard it said, "We are each born with a full keyboard. By the time we reach adulthood, we're doing well to be able to play 'Chopsticks.'" The focus for each of us is to reclaim the lost keys. We need to move back to that sacred place. We need to respond to the questions: For what has God created you? To what is God calling you?

Do we forget those questions? Do we get distracted and lose focus? Of course. All the time.

I think of Simon Peter. Following what we have come to call the Last Supper, Jesus turned to Peter to have a personal moment. For all of Peter's conviction and loyalty, Jesus knew the pressure that would be on him in the coming hours. Jesus said to him, "I have prayed for you that your own faith may not fail; and you, when once you have turned back, strengthen your brothers" (Luke 22:32).

Peter was stunned. God bless him, he then made that brash

statement about his readiness to go with Jesus to prison and even to death. Jesus calmly responded with a comment about three denials and a rooster's crow (see Luke 22:33-34). In Peter's feisty proclamation about prison and death, we know he heard the implication of Jesus' wondering if his integrity was up to the challenge. Would his integrity remain true to who he was or would it be found wanting? Jesus believed it would be the latter.

What Peter didn't hear was the affirmation. Yes, he would lose focus for a time. But then came the phrase "when once you *have turned back*," which points clearly to Jesus' belief in Peter's ultimate integrity. It is interesting that the wording "turned back" is identical in intent to the phrase "came to himself" that Jesus used in describing the pivotal turn of the prodigal son.

I have a friend who is an engineer for an airplane manufacturing company. He "keeps the wings from falling off," as I put it. I asked him what "integrity" means in his profession. He said, "It's our job to protect the structural integrity of the part. The structure has to withstand the loads to which it is subjected without failure, immediately and for the life of the structure." Isn't that the goal of living with *integrity*—to have the character to withstand the loads and pressures that life brings while remaining true to who we are without failure?

That is the goal. In reality, our wings are consistently falling off. Thus, our faith points to the importance of repentance, confession, forgiveness, and reconciliation. Our faith points to God's grace and God's conviction that we can *turn back* and *come to ourselves* again. And again.

I don't know how you will do it, but I know the importance of the search. I don't know how you will look into the mystery, discover your congruence, and find your voice, but I am confident it will include meditation, prayer, reading, journaling, reflecting, and talking openly with those you love and trust. I know that those who really seek tend to reconnect, and I know that those who reconnect experience confidence of purpose, clarity of direction, and peace. "Peace I leave with you," Jesus said, "my peace I give to you" (John 14:27).

A friend of mine had multiple battles with cancer that required a number of surgeries. The surgeries were separated with bouts of chemo and radiation. She is one of those who came out of their ordeals the stronger for having gone through them. She dedicated herself, as she put it, "to living with a greater depth of love, with more compassion to those who struggle, and with an attitude of celebration in each day of my life."

I happened to be talking with her a month or so after the tragedy of 9/11 and mentioned how many were referring to that event as a "wake-up call." With genuine surprise she said, "A wake-up call? What wake-up call? I was already awake!"

"I was already awake." Her words have remained with me. There are times in our lives when we have a sudden, horrible event happen to us or to those near us. We bolt up as if out of a sound sleep. We call it our wake-up call. We use it to reorder our priorities. We set our sails in a new direction—more spiritual, more loving, more committed to the principles in which we believe. We live with more integrity.

The question my friend's comment spurred in me was, *When do we decide to stay awake?* When do we stop having to reinvent the wheel? When do we move, as the psalmist put it, "from strength to strength" (Psalm 84:7), retaining and then building on the lessons we learned before? When?

Perhaps this time.

CHAPTER FOUR

WHO AM I *NOW*?

So if anyone is in Christ, there is a new creation: everything old has
passed away; see, everything has become new!
—2 Corinthians 5:17

We all have those times when we look at something familiar, something that has always been there, and then we
see it for the first time. My wife, Karen, and I are members of the
New Beginnings Sunday school class in our church and have
been for many years. New Beginnings—I've always liked that
name. It speaks of fresh starts, new life, sunrises.

But not long ago I looked at that same familiar name and
saw it differently. *New Beginnings*—isn't that redundant? Aren't
all beginnings new? How could you have an *old* beginning? I

didn't spend a lot of time on this idea, you understand, but it did start me wondering.

Then slowly I realized there is such a thing as an "old beginning." It happens whenever we stop growing. It's when we begin one day about the same as the day before and the day after. Each day or month or year is truly an old beginning. It's to live out, in our own way, the movie *Groundhog Day,* where every day is repeated. Lives of old beginnings are lives with marginal integrity. No longer am I in touch with who I *am*; I am only in touch with who I *was*.

Life is fluid. Changing. One phase gives way to make room for the next.

It was a warm spring morning in late May. Those gathered sat in metal chairs filling much of the quadrangle. The valedictorian had spoken from the heart, with authenticity and grace. The invited speaker spoke a little long, passing up several excellent opportunities to have concluded. The beaming graduates filed by the Headmaster, receiving their diplomas, one graduate giving the Headmaster a high five and another holding his diploma aloft for all to see that it was really there.

Graduation concluded. The air suddenly was filled with caps; a huge flock of them had taken flight. Graduates hugged, cried, and, scattering like the wind, moved into the rest of their lives.

A chapter is finished, the page is turned, and we begin to write anew.

Integrity means connecting our lives with purpose, which requires that we stay current. *Our purpose, that which gives life meaning and direction, is going to change.* We must stay current with what our purpose is now. Today. If I am still moving in a direction with an outdated purpose, I will feel an emptiness, an absence of meaning. It's like chewing a stick of Juicy Fruit gum after the "juicy fruit" is gone—all I have left is gum.

Integrity requires new beginnings, not old ones, as we live lives that are moving forward. At any one time many of us are in the process of a significant life change. It may be subtle, unacknowledged, perhaps even subconscious. Yet we are moving ahead with a new purpose, taking us in a new direction, from which we can discover lives of meaning and fulfillment.

AN INTUITIVE CALL

Transition is often inspired by a sense of *call*, an intuitive spiritual, emotional awareness that it is time for that page to be turned; it is time for this chapter to end and the new to begin. It is a call into that next phase of our lives. "Everything old has passed away; see, everything has become new!" (2 Corinthians 5:17). *Life transition* is God's continuing creation.

Do you remember one of those tugs from a time in your past? Perhaps it was when you were called into a new venture or a new career or a volunteer opportunity. It may have begun with a feeling of unrest. It is the feeling that you have outgrown where you have been. You feel the uneasiness, the restlessness. It is time to move on. Often this begins with some discomfort, a time of anxiety or mild depression, when I know that where I have been—and where I still am—no longer fits. We experience it as being *time for a change*.

Integrity involves both knowing who God created me to be and what God is calling me to be about—right now, at this moment in my life. Integrity asks the question, "Who am I?" Integrity in times of transition asks, "Who am I *now*?" Who am I in this new place, in this new time of my life?

Knowing who I am is an issue of self-identity. Knowing who I am at any point in my life is an issue of ongoing discernment. The principles and values that define us are basically in place. They will be tweaked and refined, but they rarely change substantially. How we apply those values, and which of them are given priority at any particular point in our lives, is open to our ongoing intuitive discrimination.

Integrity implies that we are growing and discerning anew who and where we are, and in what direction we are now going. I have always valued psychologist Sheldon Kopp's books, and I've also enjoyed his book titles. He entitled his book about change and the ongoing process of life *Here I Am, Wasn't I!* Our lives are fluid. We are in motion.

Those activities and interests that were center stage at one point may hardly be on my radar screen at another. "Been there, done that," as they say. What filled my life with meaning and purpose may be a fond memory, but it no longer has the vitality or power that it once did.

A friend of mine had extensive surgery requiring bed rest for several weeks. She was both a wise and brilliant woman who used the time for thoughtful, personal reflection. There were several insights she gained. One was the awareness of all the activities in which she was involved simply because, at an earlier point in her life, she had said "yes." These involvements had been meaningful and fulfilling when she had begun, because of where she was in her life at that time. They *had been*, but were no longer. She resolved to reevaluate every few months, to see what still had meaning for her and what she wanted to continue—and what had lost its purpose for her now that she needed to let go.

The scriptures consistently encourage new beginnings. "Do not be conformed to this world, but be transformed by the renewing of your minds, so that you may discern what is the will of God" (Romans 12:2). *Be transformed,* meaning "to change the form," by the ongoing renewing of our minds. New beginnings. Persons willing to be created anew by discerning the will of God for their lives.

Life transitions—at least those not forced upon us—begin with a subtle call, which leads to reflection, which leads to the opportunity to change. *Transition equals call, reflection, and change. Every personal passage is* unique, yet most have these elements in common. They don't always come in a set sequence, but these elements tend to be there.

A little hand slipped quietly into hers. They walked together, got their sack lunches, and picked out a tree for a picnic.

Some nation called the Republic of Georgia hadn't been on her radar screen. She had barely heard of it. But she had felt a yearning for something new, something different in her life just as the invitation had come to her. Successful, talented, affluent, respected in her field— whatever. It was meaning she wanted, and it was meaning she didn't have. There was no meaning because there was no purpose.

Yes. She said yes. She would be glad to go to some forsaken place and help build a bathroom for kids in an orphanage. Her hands, which had never known a hard day's work, were carrying cement blocks, mixing mortar, and assisting those who knew what they were doing. At the end of the third or fourth day she stretched out on her cot and laughed as she remembered the words of an elderly African-American woman at the end of a civil rights march: "My feets is tired, but my soul is rested." Her soul felt more rested and at peace than it had in years.

Her job had been to help build a bathroom. As

always, she was focused on her task. She was kind, even gracious to those around her, but consistently she had tunnel vision. So she didn't notice when her warmth touched the hungry heart of a small girl. Quietly she had a second shadow as she went through each day. Never intrusive, but ever-present.

Then, as they broke for lunch one day, she felt the grasp of that little hand in hers—and both hearts were touched. Every day, from then on, it was just the two of them for lunch. No one else was invited. The same two, the same tree.

Meaning. As she had never known it.

A TIME OF REFLECTION

Most of life's major transitions allow us advance notice. Many are of our choosing. They begin with *a call*, followed by— if time allows—*a time of reflection.*

In transitions of our choosing, this is where they begin. The focus may be on our career, our relationships, our lifestyles, our spirituality, or whatever of significance in our lives is no longer working well. As soon as we are aware that we *need to make a change*, transition begins. It's a time to discern, a time to let *what will be* emerge.

Integrity is central to this process. How I feel, what I think, and what I do must be congruent. How I feel—the direction to which I feel led—and what I think—factoring in what *makes sense*—lead me to where I want to go.

Again, the words of Paul: "Do not be conformed to this world, but be transformed by the renewing of your minds, so that you may discern what is the will of God" (Romans 12:2). Paul begins by discounting what *this world* might choose or what it might think of your decision. This is your life, and this decision is in your hands.

It is then, he writes, a time of *renewal*—here is this idea of new beginnings. *Renewing of your mind.* Doesn't that point to throwing open the shutters of our imaginations to whatever new possibilities might be on the horizon? Implied in this is to stop doing what we have always done "just because"...well, just because that's the way we've always done it.

It is a time to find my voice. My own voice. It is a time to *discern what is the will of God* for me at this point in my life. What is my purpose at this moment? It is a time of discovery of who I am now and where I am headed. To what do I feel called? Integrity.

It is a time to find "what is *good and acceptable and perfect*" (Romans 12:2, emphasis added). What is good for me—what I discern feels right; what is acceptable—what makes sense; what is perfect—in the sense of "perfect wholeness" to my life.

The image of being in a canoe on a rushing mountain stream always comes to mind. I am looking for the flow, the direction of my life. When I lose my way, I find I am paddling cross-current or even struggling to go upstream. When I am living with integrity, I am in the flow of the life designed for me.

This period of reflection goes by different names. It has been called the "Fertile Void."[19] Others call it "the neutral zone."[20] It is a time when we are out of gear, not pushing forward. As Thomas Merton put it, "[I]t seems to me that I have greater peace and am close to God when I am not 'trying to be a contemplative,' or trying to be anything special, but simply orienting my life fully and completely towards what seems to be required of a man like me at a time like this."[21]

As we are deciding what we are to be about, we let the land lie fallow for a season, as the farmers would say. Remember when you have struggled to think of a name or a word? The harder you tried, the farther it seemed to slip away. Then you moved on to other things, got distracted...and boom, it came to you. This is akin to letting your future, the next direction in your life, lie fallow for a time. If you feel stuck in the process, stop working so hard at it. *Many of life's most important decisions are not made, they are discovered.* Let it lie fallow for a season. Yet, as my wife cautions, we need to make sure we are lying fallow and not just lying—immobilized, lacking the courage or motivation to decide.

For some, this time of reflection is rather peaceful. Naturally, there is the sense of unease as change is in the air. There is the emptiness that prompts the need for transition. But the tone is quiet and reflective.

For others this time of reflection is not quite so mellow. Instead of it feeling like a *fertile void*, it's more like *fertile chaos*. Panic, even. It can be frightening. There is the rumbling awareness that there is going to be change—big change—and its exact nature is unknown. The old is passing away. The new is not yet in sight.

We can understand why chaos has always gotten such bad press. It is uncomfortable. It puts us out of control. We don't know where it will lead or leave us. Yet in the midst of all the turmoil that sometimes accompanies transition, growth happens. In fact, growth may know no more fertile ground than those white-knuckle eras of our life stories when we are feeling lost and so alone. As the old cliché goes, "The acorn, as it is cracking and being split apart, likely doesn't know it is becoming an oak tree."

The woman stands at her bedroom window. She holds the curtain back so she can better see for the final time. The garden in the backyard still looks lovely, though not quite as kept as when they could tend it together. His death was such a loss in so many ways. They were quite a team. After all this time she can still hear his laughter and feel the rough but loving touch of his hand.

She hears a noise, lets go of the curtain, turns and almost stumbles over one of the boxes that litters the floor of what has been their home. It's the moving van. She blinks back her tears and walks toward the door.

CAUTIONS

In these times of discernment and reflection, many struggle with impatience. Let me remind those of us who are proactive, high energy, Type A: this isn't a process that can be hurried. It takes time. The Spirit does indeed move as it will. We do everything we can to facilitate—tend the soil, plant the seeds—and then we wait.

Take your time. Don't hurry. You are discovering who you are at this moment in your life. You are discerning your deepest, most soulful direction. Give yourself to the process. Accept the pace as natural and healthy. Don't hurry it. Don't fight it.

I have always heard that the exodus Moses led from Egypt could have taken less than three weeks. If the Israelites had taken a direct northeasterly course, they could have made it that quickly. Instead, they crossed the sea, hung a mean right for Mt. Sinai, and it took them forty years. God knew they needed the time. The time for reflection. The time to learn, to grow—the time to discover and to claim their new identity. If they had taken the shortcut, they indeed would have been in Canaan; but for them, as a people, it would not have been the Promised Land.

What you are about is so important. There is a powerful quotation attributed to Jesus contained in the noncanonical collection of sayings known as the Gospel of Thomas:

"If you bring forth what is within you, what you bring forth will save you. If you do not bring forth what is within you, what you do not bring forth will destroy you."[22]

You may be discerning some of the deepest and most fundamental questions of your life. "Who am I now?" "Where do I want to go with my life?" These are the questions. Give them time. Live with them. Let the answers emerge. This is tough for those of us who are "ready, fire, aim" people, but we have to respect that taking the time to aim is essential.

Take your time—but don't obsess. *Obsessing* is intensely ruminating over and over in ways that aren't productive. It doesn't get traction. It is filled with anxiety and often is trying to force an awareness. It lacks the feel of reflection, of patience, of discovery. Obsessing wants to induce labor before the baby is ready to be born, and ironically it tends to interrupt and delay the process.

Another danger to avoid is trying to skew the results with what you would *like* for them to be. Don't you love the way Susan B. Anthony said it? "I distrust those people who know so well what God wants them to do, because I notice it always coincides with their own desires."[23]

What I experience and think of as "God's call" is always congruent with what is best for me. But it may not be what I consciously *want* at a more superficial level of my experience of myself.

Abraham Lincoln cautioned us not to be looking for God to endorse what we already want, implying God is on our side. Rather, said Lincoln, "We should pray and worry earnestly whether we are on God's side."[24] Many of our motives are based on subconscious defenses and insecurities. We may have developed a lifestyle too devoted to protecting us from interests and involvements that may take us outside our realm of comfort. Like Moses in the glow of that remarkable burning bush, we may resist.

I once heard it said, in regard to reading a passage of scripture, to "stay with it until it surprises you." Don't settle for the obvious or for what you want it to say. Stay with it until it surprises you—until you are enriched with a new awareness. Stay with this process of discernment until it surprises you. Stay with it until you have a new awareness of who you are and where you are headed. It likely will not be where you began.

A final thought about reflection: don't be surprised or dismayed if you feel a time of depression. You may well experience what classically has been referred to as "the workshop of the soul." We go down into the depths to digest, to process something new in our lives. Transition always involves processing the new and may leave you feeling momentarily less connected, less energized, less focused—in other words, mildly depressed. Assuming the depression isn't severe and that it doesn't last, it simply means you have gone down to the basement to spend some time in the workshop of your soul.

MAKING THE CHANGE

Transition involves taking seriously the call, engaging the time of reflection, and then making the change. *Transition is the internal process. Change is the resulting action.*[25] Pulling the trigger on what you have decided has the most integrity for you may be a moment of exhilaration or anxiety or terror. Your reaction depends on who you are and what you have decided. This change may be engaged easily or it may require courage. Do it. Follow your heart. Whatever you discerned, do it. Whatever path is best for you, follow it.

Making the change is actually a two-part process. We begin with *the ending*—the ending to *what was*. It's the "goodbye" that must precede the welcome into the new life. A graduation ceremony, a moving van, a retirement party, a funeral—these are some obvious symbols of those endings. Some endings are formalized into rituals. Most are far more subtle.

It had been their ritual for exactly a decade. While Mama handed out candy at the front door, Daddy had the privilege of escorting their little girl around the neighborhood trick-or-treating. For him it was nothing but a treat, a sheer joy. He would wait curbside, with flashlight in hand, as she went up to the door, rang the bell, and announced the all-too-familiar words.

A princess, a cheerleader, Snow White, even a hippie one year. So many costumes as the years had gone by. And the years had flown by. She was much taller now.

It happened on a stretch of their street with darkened houses and little distraction. As they walked, she said, "Daddy, you know this will be our last year. I'll be too old to do this next time."

He had to catch his breath. He knew it was coming, but just the same… "I know, darlin'. But hasn't it been a great run?"

She let go of his hand as she ran to the next house and rang the bell.

The ending is that turning of the page from the former chapter of our lives. Mitch Albom said it well: "All endings are beginnings . . . we just don't know it at the time."

The scriptures guide us beautifully here:

> *Do not remember the former things,*
> *or consider the things of old,*
> I am about to do a new thing;
> now it springs forth, do you not perceive it?
> I will make a way in the wilderness
> and rivers in the desert.
>
> (Isaiah 43:18-19, emphasis added)

How clearly the scripture is saying, it's time to end it. Close the chapter that is now finished. Say goodbye to the things of old, so we can be about doing *a new thing*.

Endings. Pause for just a moment, and just read the word. *Endings.* Don't you feel a sadness just letting the word settle into your awareness? Endings involve losses. Even when the change is longed for and sought, there are new relationships, routines, patterns of living that make life feel as though home will never be quite the same again.

Some may get too emotionally engulfed with the ending, but most who err will want to avoid the emotions—altogether, if possible. "You've got to leave the past in the past and move on," as I have heard it said so many times. Yet the best way *not* to leave the past in the past is to prematurely try to leave the past in the past. Did you get that? Let me say it more succinctly: if I'm not finished with it, I'll take it with me.

If I'm feeling sadness about the ending, I've got to give it a voice. I've got to get it out. I have to find my way of expressing it. It may be through letting out my tears, talking it out with one who cares, openly saying my *goodbyes*, or putting it down on paper.

If I have been transferred with my company and I'm moving halfway across the country, simply saying, "Aw, we'll be getting together" to someone who really matters to me may not suffice. *Maybe* we'll be getting together, or maybe both of our lives will become so busy that we never do. The slap on the back along with the remark "I'll be seeing you down the road" may be simply the avoidance of doing what has greater integrity in such moments—expressing it. Looking each other in the eye and saying goodbye. Saying out loud—*in front of God and everybody*—how much the relationship means.

I am always hearing about "closure." I never really cared for the word. It obviously implies closing something. What I am describing is not closing, but *finishing, completing.* As I say goodbye, as I acknowledge the importance of my friend having been in my life, I have both a personal moment in that relationship, and I take a step toward turning the page.

Or perhaps my goodbye is not to a person but to a place, a task, a dream, or a vocation. Give a voice to how you feel.

If we don't take seriously the need to acknowledge the passage, we may make the external "change" without making the internal "transition"—leaving us with new circumstances but still *back there* with old longings and loose ends. Transition involves attitude and emotion at least as much as behavior. Again, integrity is all three: thinking, feeling, and acting.

Paul wrote of personal growth to the church in Corinth. He pointed to the necessary ending required as we "put an end to childish ways" in order to become fully the adults we are intended to be (1 Corinthians 13:11).

When Jesus spoke of the growth of intimacy in marriage, he began with the ending: "For this reason a man shall leave his father and mother and be joined to his wife, and the two shall become one flesh" (Mark 10:7-8). One chapter has to end; the parents no longer come first. The page has to be turned for the new one to begin.

It was rather a coincidence. Of their good friends, six couples were becoming empty nesters at the same time. They planned a party for the last Saturday in August.

All six sons and daughters had just been moved into their dorm rooms. There was much laughter as refreshments were sipped and hors d'oeuvres passed around. Comparisons were made between how much "stuff" girls took to college versus boys. Actually, it was determined there was no comparison. In the midst of the noise there was a quiet moment here and there as a brief story was told of a tender goodbye outside a college dorm.

It was time to eat. They went into the dining room and took their places. There they found at the head of each place-setting two symbols of their evening—a small package of Kleenex and a travel brochure.

To acknowledge the endings means to give a voice to the loss and to celebrate the joy.

THE NEW BEGINNING

The arrival on the far side is *our new beginning*. If the ending is like a death, the beginning is the new life. This is the new shore to which this journey takes us.

Your new beginning may involve fireworks and a band, or more likely, as with mine, it will slip quietly into your awareness. One day an event may jog us, and we realize, "So this is where I am now." Or perhaps you say to yourself, "Now I am ready, and this is where I want to go." We have discovered our new purpose. With it will come direction, and from it we will find meaning.

Life, at its best, is a process. We never arrive and permanently set up camp. We are changing, growing. We need new beginnings.

Note how the psalmist put it:

Happy are those whose strength is in you,
> in whose heart are the highways to Zion.
As they go through the valley of Baca
> they make it a place of springs;
> the early rain also covers it with pools.
They go from strength to strength;
> the God of gods will be seen in Zion.
> Psalm 84:5-7 (emphasis added)

"They go from strength to strength." They keep moving forward—learning, growing—moving from strength to strength. When the discernment has been made, when the choice has been selected, go for it. It is the only move that has integrity. My thinking and my feeling must then be matched by my actions.

Make your decision, and don't second-guess yourself. Don't allow doubts and fears to overcome what you have courageously decided. Make the difficult decision, and move forward with your life.

Know there will be internal resistance. In *The Life We Are Given*, George Leonard and Michael Murphy put it this way: "Every one of us resists significant change, no matter whether it's for the worse or for the better. Our body, brain, and behavior have a built-in tendency to stay the same within rather narrow limits and to snap back when changed."[26] We resist change. The old way may be less preferable, but it is familiar, and there is value there. The new way is foreign and unfamiliar, and therefore it seems risky.

There will be fears about this new, foreign territory you are entering. There will be anxiety about the rightness of this new direction. There will be sadness about leaving the old, leaving the way it was.

There are those who never make the full transition. Following widowhood, divorce, or retirement, many find themselves either living in the past or stuck with feelings from the past. Some idealize "the way it was" so that the present can never successfully compare to the past. As one husband was heard to say, "There are two perfect men who have ever lived: Jesus Christ and my wife's first husband, who died."

For people who can't quite make the transition, the talk is too often of the past. There is the clear sense that those were the glory days, they are over, and that there is no motivation to find what is glorious about *these* days. Life around them goes on, but within their heart of hearts something remains frozen, arrested.

Gail Godwin spoke to this in her novel, *The Finishing School*:

> "There are two kinds of people," she once decreed to me emphatically. "One kind, you can just tell by looking at them at what point they congealed into their final selves. It might be a very nice self, but you know you can expect no more surprises from it. Whereas, the other kind keep moving, changing....They are fluid. They keep moving forward and making new trysts with life, and the motion of it keeps them young. In my opinion, they are the only people who are still alive. You must be constantly on your guard, Justin, against congealing."[27]

Congealing is such a perfect word. It's like a wobbling dish of Jell-O: it looks alive—but, of course, it's as dead as a brick. Many look alive, but they've quit growing. They've congealed. They have not completed an important transition. They may have settled into "a very nice self," but the life, vitality, and meaning are somehow gone. So much of who they are has become dormant.

Life cannot be lived in the past tense.

Lot's wife is the poster child for this behavior. You just can't help but think of her in this context, can you? She turned to look back to Sodom and Gomorrah and instantly became a pillar of salt (see Genesis 19:1-29; Luke 17:28-33). In wanting to hang on to the life she had known, she was refusing to move on to the next step in her life journey. She always would live not just *with* her memories but *in* her memories. She would hang on to what had been at the expense of what was to come. There would be no new beginnings, only old ones. She "congealed."

Many of you are beginning new chapters from changes that are not of your choosing. Perhaps you have had to accept a death or a divorce. You have been powerless, out of control. You have taken a major hit. But now you have a measure of power back. You have choice.

A friend of mine, whose husband had died years before, said to me, "I finally had to acknowledge that along with the tragedy of his death, I am now single and free to do whatever I choose to do with my life." That freedom may seem insignificant compared to the magnitude of your loss, but you have the freedom to choose.

Judy squeezed his hand for all she was worth and gave a final push.

Finally their baby was arriving. "Here it comes!" the doctor all but shouted. "It's a—it's a girl!"

There was a feeling of such excitement, in the midst of professionals quickly doing their jobs. They joined this young couple in welcoming their dream. As the physician cut the cord, she continued, "She's here. You two kids are now parents..."

And then there was silence.

The doctor looked at the baby as she held her. Having delivered thousands of infants, she knew.... Tests would have to be done, but she knew. Quietly she handed this precious bundle to a nurse. Without a word she slipped off her gloves, took the new father by the arm, and escorted him into the hallway. Puzzled but totally focused, he took in every word.

"Your daughter looks healthy. But she will have limitations. There is a disability. She has Down syndrome."

He heard little else. The doctor may have said something about her telling Judy in a few minutes, and maybe something about the need for him to be strong for his wife. But mostly it was a blur.

This gentle doctor gave him a hug and went back to the delivery room. With eyes unfocused, he stared ahead. Slowly he began to walk down the hallway. Tears were now welling. Quietly he cried as he looked out the window, seeing nothing—but feeling far too much.

Several minutes passed. He stared into the distance— his mind racing with thoughts and questions, his heart filled with pain and disappointment for the challenges his little girl would face.

Slowly he came back into focus. He looked down the hallway and said to himself, "Well—this isn't the child I expected, but now it's time to let that child go and meet our daughter."

You have the power to choose what is best for you and what is next for you. Robert Louis Stevenson said, "Life often isn't a matter of being dealt good cards but of playing a poor hand well." You have been dealt a new hand—not necessarily a poor one, but a different one. Look at the cards you now are holding. Play them intentionally, and play them well.

PART II

MORAL INTEGRITY:
A PERSON OF VALUES

Do not be weary in doing what is right.
2 Thessalonians 3:13

Adolf Hitler is a man whose name inevitably enters any meaningful discussion of integrity. Why? Because in believing Jews were evil, in hating them, in murdering them, Adolf Hitler's thinking, his feeling, and his acting were congruent. He met, it would seem, the guidelines for integrity. Could it be—Adolf Hitler, the personification of evil, acted with integrity?

Not so fast.

Earlier in this writing we discussed *two* meanings of integrity—both of which are required. The first is *personal* integrity, from the Latin *integer*, meaning "whole, complete." This half of the meaning has been our focus up to this point. And the answer is, *yes,* Hitler's thinking, feeling, and acting do seem to be congruent. But his life was anything but a life of integrity.

The second half of integrity is *moral* integrity. *The Oxford English Dictionary* defines this side of integrity as meaning "soundness of moral principle; the character of uncorrupted virtue, esp. in relation to truth and fair dealing; uprightness, honest, sincerity."[1] That sets the bar high, the virtues we seek as we aspire to lives of integrity. Then *Webster's Third New International Dictionary* adds a tone of caution, as it also defines integrity as avoiding "deception, expediency, artificiality or shallowness."[2]

Not just any belief or principle will pass muster for a life of integrity. It comes from a character of uncorrupted virtue, based on *truth, fair dealing, and uprightness.* Moral integrity points to lives with depth, wisdom, and sincerity that would be incongruent with motives based on *deception, expediency, artificiality, or shallowness.*

In a terribly pathological way, Hitler may have passed the consistency test; but when we apply to his life the standards of moral integrity, he failed on every level.

To live with integrity means that I live with authenticity and congruence, and that I live a *moral life* with authenticity and congruence.

In this section we turn to the moral dimension of integrity. If I stand as an authentic person, I need something for which I stand. Moral integrity comprises the values, the virtues, the principles that define me.

FROM CUSTOMS TO VALUES

At the heart of moral integrity is the conviction that there are objective values. There are attitudes and behaviors that are superior to others. Those we hold in the highest regard are the ones to which we aspire.

The history of morality and values is an interesting evolution. The words *moral* and *morality* that represent these values to which we aspire come from the Latin word *mores*. This origin simply means "custom"—pointing to what the customs were or what was customarily done. There was no value judgment given, no qualitative right or wrong assessed. *Mores* means "this is the way things are usually done around here."

Out of *customs* come morals and values. Societies place valuations on them regarding which of these practices is of greater or lesser value—which is good or bad, right or wrong, healthy or unhealthy. How these are distinguished has been the focus of philosophers, theologians, and ethicists at least since the time of Plato and Aristotle, three centuries before Christ.

There are a variety of ways the great thinkers have approached morality. At one extreme are ethical nihilists who see no inherent moral values, and ethical relativists who see each individual or society as defining values for themselves. Morals for them, therefore, have no objective standard, but are simply in the eyes of the beholder.[3]

Yet for many ethical thinkers—certainly those who are persons of faith—there is the conviction that a desire for morality is a part of our common human nature. There is a core desire for goodness and for the welfare of those around us. Paul wrote to this point in his letter to the Romans: those who do not possess the law "show that what the law requires is written on their hearts, to which their own conscience also bears witness" (2:15).

UNIVERSAL VALUES

Not only does there seem to be this common, hard-wired desire for morality, there are also clear parallels in the specific values of those who are thoughtful and wise around the world. I could quote Gandhi, the Dalai Lama, Elie Wiesel, and Mother Teresa on the same theme—people who espouse similar values, yet who come from such different backgrounds.

There appears to be a common reference in beginning this discernment of values. Not surprisingly, this shared reference point is consistently expressed in the world's religions.

Several years ago an especially tragic event happened in Atlanta. A man had a psychotic break and murdered his family and several work colleagues. Most of the deaths occurred in an office building just around the corner from our church. A memorial service was planned by the church, and the city of Atlanta requested that it be a community-wide event to remember the lives of those who had been lost.

The nine persons who died represented a remarkable cross section of the world's religions. A clergyperson from each of these faith groups was invited to speak at the service. As it turned out, they all took a part of their time to talk about the values and virtues to which their faiths aspire. We were truly sitting with sisters and brothers, though from differing backgrounds. A friend asked me after the service, "Greer, did you hear that Hindu speak?" I knew exactly to what he was referring. We had all been riveted as this kind, soft-spoken man had talked with gripping compassion of grace, acceptance, and love. My buddy continued, "Heck, he sounded more Christian than the two of us put together."

Never before had it come so sharply into focus for me. For all the differences in the various faiths, when it comes to the values of how we are to be in relationship with each other and our world, they are notably similar. Compassion, truthfulness, humility, kindness, justice, tolerance, and avoiding harm are emphasized across virtually every religion.

STARTING POINTS

We now turn to the question, Where do we begin in discerning those values that have integrity for us? Where is our starting point? If this is to be well done, it is crucial that it be well begun. If our direction is flawed, we can travel for miles and be no closer to where our integrity calls us.

As philosopher Louis Pojman outlines, the values I adopt become the foundation for the principles by which I live. Those principles then frame my judgments that guide my decisions which result in my actions.[4]

My moral life—from my principles,

to my judgments,

to my decisions,

to my actions—

begins with those values.

If you know who you are, you will know what to do.

Where is our starting point in arriving at our moral base? For most of us, there are two.

Naturally, it is first from the values with which we are reared. We can try to sound profound about this, but it is simply from the lessons learned in the den of our childhood homes. From that first "No" and "Now, that's a good boy," we began incorporating values into our young lives. These are both the lessons we explicitly were taught and—more important—the lessons modeled for us as we watched those with whom we lived.

We later may have accepted those lessons with little critique or completely rebelled against them. More likely, we—intuitively or thoughtfully—appraised each lesson for the worth we saw in it, kept those lessons that had integrity for us, and moved on from the rest. It is always of interest for the parents of any college student to learn on those visits home which of the traditional life lessons have continued to pass muster, which have been refined, and which no longer compute. The students are claiming those values that have integrity for them. Refining what we believe hopefully will continue. Sharpening this focus is a lifelong process for those who want to grow.

A second moral starting point is from the teachings of our faith. Just as those childhood values must have a personal congruence, it is also necessary that they are congruent with the values at the heart of our religious teachings.

My faith is Christian. Likely the same is true for most persons reading this. Values that are Christian form the core of our moral lives. We believe that the clearest window into the heart of God is the life and teachings of Jesus Christ. What he taught and the example he gave become the starting point of our faith. They begin with love, compassion, forgiveness, hope, reconciliation, and humility. Those values push us to acts of charity and kindness and do not allow us to sit passively in the face of injustice or wrong in any of its forms.

A distinction is important here between *values* and *virtues*. Most think of the terms as synonymous. They are closely related, yet there is a difference. *Values* point to attitudes and actions. Values are the beliefs and ideals we consider to be important in our lives. Values are the principles and the behaviors we hold to be—well—valuable. *Virtues* are even more personal. *Virtues* are the qualities of character and moral excellence within us. They point to the fundamentals of our moral character ingrained over time. Whereas an *attitude* is a value, an *attribute* is a virtue. If we admire courage, then courage is one of our values. If we are courageous, then courage is one of our virtues.

The church has long identified and emphasized virtues as the ideals to which we aspire. Historically the church has had a list of "the seven virtues." Technically there have been a couple of versions, but with much overlap. The list that is most common includes faith, hope, love, courage (or fortitude), justice, prudence, and temperance. The other well-known historic list, referred to as the Seven Contrary Virtues, matches each of the seven deadly sins with a corrective virtue.

Granted, we've updated some of the terms, but as Christians these are the types of virtues for which we stand. Though this is what we believe, we work to be sensitive and understanding of others' points of view. We work not to impose our beliefs on equally valid, though differing, views—which comes from our value of respect.

Yet we can't be so sheepishly sensitive to differing opinions that we fail to advocate the moral virtues and values at the core of who we are and what we believe. We can't go from restraint in imposing beliefs to devaluing our values. *Anything* doesn't go.

There *are* rights and wrongs. Being respectful, kind, truthful, and loving is preferable to being rude, hostile, self-centered, and dishonest. The Christian faith emphasizes this. Religions around the world confirm it. Reason and common sense support it. These are core values. We must advocate these with clarity and conviction—though without a rigidity that closes our ears or our minds or our hearts.

We begin with being grounded in what is right, in the values in which we believe. However, from that point our quest for moral integrity has only begun. How we interpret those values, how we give them priority, how we apply them with each of our personalities to the unique situations we encounter—all of this has to be considered. We must sort out which values are important for our focus in this particular context.

We have returned to discernment. With the guidance of God's grace, we each have to discover and claim the values that we decide will be the basis of how we will live our lives. Then we have to discern how we will give priority to those values and apply them to real-life situations. As Parker Palmer wrote, "Before you tell your life what truths and values you have decided to live up to, let your life tell you what truths you embody, what values you represent."[5]

I once heard of a monastery in which the monks were asked to reflect each day on the question, *What is precious to you?*

Which values *are* precious to you? Which virtues? On which would you bet your life? On which *do* you bet your life? By which is your life defined?

A few years back it became popular among young Christians to wear WWJD bracelets. It was a reminder to ask, What would Jesus do? *prior to making any moral or ethical decision. What could be finer than to wonder what Jesus would do if faced with this life situation? Yet that question, to me, is just the starting point. I had an idea for another bracelet—and no, it never would have caught on. Mine would have read WWGHMD: What would God have me do? I'm not Jesus.*

When it comes to values and moral living, Jesus is clearly my most important and influential teacher. His lessons are my primary reference point. But that is not going to let me off the hook of discerning the values to which I am called. He had his unique personality, and I have mine. He had his calling, and I have mine.

Wondering what Jesus might do if faced with my life

decision will point me in a direction that is morally sound. But then I have to decide *what God would have me do* with this personality, in this context, in this life for which I have been created and to which I feel called.

If you know who you are, you'll know what to do.

It is interesting to note that the word *values* and its first cousin, *value* (as in "the assignment of worth to something"), come from the Latin word *ualere*, meaning "to be strong, hence well."[6] I have an interest, as you surely have noticed, in the origin of words. I believe in the theory that the genesis of a word usually remains at the core of its meaning as it evolves over the centuries. If this is true, then "to be strong (and) well" is to take seriously one's values—to give them priority, to assign them worth, and to give them a place at the table where decisions are made and life is lived.

LEVELS OF MORAL MOTIVATION

What I am encouraging calls for a high level of moral functioning. Lawrence Kohlberg developed a model outlining six stages of moral development grouped into three moral levels.

His focus is largely on children's developmental stages and at which points they can attain higher levels of moral functioning. For our purposes, his levels provide a guide to how far we have grown and from which motivation we make moral judgments.

The first of Kohlberg's three moral levels, Level I, is pretty basic. It is to do the right thing because it's good for me—I avoid punishment, or I get rewarded. Level II moves outside my self-absorption to focus on the world around me. This motivation to do the right thing is to uphold "the rules and expectations and conventions of society or authority just because they are society's rules, expectations, or conventions."[7] Those who make judgments at this level don't tend to raise questions or think things through in much detail. They genuinely want to do what is good and pleasing and allow that to be defined outside of them—accepting the customs of their community and following them.

Level III, the highest level, is also to understand society's rules, but to appreciate the principles and values behind them as well. At this level one chooses what is right not out of self-interest or a blind adherence to conventions but out of a reflective, thoughtful conviction believing in the principles that make it right. This is the level to which we aspire. Our focus here is on the values, on what we hold to be true, on the principles that guide our rules and our actions.

If you know who you are...

STARTING FROM HERE

We each must begin from where we are if we are to grow in our moral integrity. If we really want to know what our values are, we shouldn't look at our mission statements. They contain our goals and aspirations, not necessarily our real values. If we want to discover our genuine values, we must look at how we live.

Look at what we do when no one's looking, when no one will ever know. Look at how we treat those who have no authority or impact in our lives—whose paths we likely will never cross again. Those are the choices we make when there is no one to impress, no image to maintain. That is where we each will find, for better or worse, what we really believe. There we find who we really are.

This awareness of our real selves is crucial. I cannot grow from where I wish I were or hope to be. I can only grow from where I am. I must be honest with myself. That is the only place from which I can begin. And if I discover that my moral bar is set disappointingly low—if how I live is incongruent with what I believe—then I have life-changing decisions before me. Just as personal integrity involves a congruence with my thoughts, feelings, and actions, moral integrity holds a similar congruence with what I believe and how I live.

Our principles and values constitute much of what makes up our core as persons. Because of our commitments to the values we have chosen, we become persons of substance. Therefore, it is vital to make those choices well—with intentionality and wisdom. As author J. K. Rowling has Dumbledore say to his student Harry Potter, "It's our choices, Harry, that show what we truly are, far more than our abilities."[8]

> *Bobby Jones would define himself as a golfer when he won the Grand Slam of golf. He defined himself as a person, to most of the public, at the 1925 U.S. Open.*
>
> *He was playing the eleventh hole at Worcester Country Club outside Boston. Before his pitch to the green, Jones believed he had inadvertently caused the ball to move ever so slightly—a violation of the rules. He turned to one of the marshals and called the penalty on himself. Discussion then followed among the officials.*

Neither the marshals nor his playing partner, Walter Hagen, had seen the ball move. Hagen tried to dissuade him from pressing the point. When he finished his round, officials continued discouraging him from assessing the penalty. There was no changing his mind. He knew what he saw. His score was a 77, not a 76.

The violation was a stroke penalty. With that stroke he would have won the U.S. Open.

As impressive as the integrity of that decision, his comment to a friend after the tournament was equally striking. He was being appropriately praised for the character and sportsmanship he had shown. Jones seemed surprised and even indignant at the attention he was getting for simply following the rules. He said, "You'd as well praise me for not breaking into banks."[9]

LIFE GETS COMPLICATED

Anchored; we must be anchored in what we believe. To meet the challenges of living in this world, we have to know our values.

We will face difficult situations that will require choices of us. Yes or no. Up or down. One way or the other. We will have to decide, and then we will live with that decision. The values we have chosen will be our basis.

Life will throw us curves. It will be essential to be grounded, but it will not be enough just to know what we believe. We will have to decide which of those values most appropriately apply in any given situation. The tests life gives us are rarely true/false— they are almost always multiple choice, with many choices. Life is often lived in the gray.

Then, just to complicate matters further, life will present complex problems in which we not only have to know our values and which ones apply but also in which we find our values to be in conflict with one another, so that we have to give them priority. One value will take us one way. Another one, equally valid, will guide us the other way. Which value should be given the greater weight?

Living with moral integrity can be difficult—at times, *really* difficult. The choices may be equally important, equally valid. They involve trade-offs, corresponding advantages and disadvantages.

For example, the cancer has returned: do you go for another

round of gut-wrenching chemotherapy or opt for quality of living in what likely will be the last few months of life?

Or say you learned that over the past decade your business partner, a friend for years, had embezzled hundreds of thousands of dollars from you to cover gambling debts. What would you do? Fire him? Have him arrested? Keep him on as he begins to repay a fraction of what he has taken? Forgive both him and the debt?

Or what if the school in your district is substandard. Your child is bright, and you want to give her every chance to succeed in life. Private school is not an affordable option. Then it dawns on you, your parents live in the district of a school with an outstanding reputation. The question comes into focus: Should you lie to the school board about your daughter's place of residence? Should you tell them she lives at her grandparents' address? What do you do?

Living with moral integrity isn't easy.

Jesus dealt with dilemmas as the Pharisees challenged him about violating Jewish law. Though the law dictated that no work was to be done on the Sabbath, Jesus would be presented with someone to be healed, when the act of healing, in and of itself, would be considered doing work—a dilemma between conflicting values. With Jesus, compassion won. And the Pharisees, with their expected rigidity, slammed him. "You hypocrites!" Jesus began, answering his critics with a notable lack of subtlety. "Does not each of you on the sabbath untie his ox or his donkey from the manger, and lead it away to give it water? And ought not this woman...be set free from this bondage on the sabbath day?" (Luke 13:15-16).

Dueling values: we are faced with them countless times. From among the relevant values, we have to select which is more important. Which is more important in this moment, in this context? Which has the greater integrity? We all have to decide for ourselves.

Living with integrity isn't easy. When there is a cost to the clear choice that we know is right, we bite the bullet and pay the price. But when the choice isn't so clear, it is even tougher. When there are competing values, we discern and make our decision—but often with an uneasiness. In giving preference to one value over another, we may have chosen wisely, but in that decision we have had to override the value we did not choose. We have had to deny a value we had claimed was important to us. We may know it was the correct choice, know it was made with wisdom, but still we may walk away with a nagging guilt or anxiety that we have just betrayed one of our values. Not all decisions made with integrity feel good.

Again, we first must be anchored in those virtues and values that define the quality and direction of our lives. That is our foundation. We must claim what we believe—the values to which we aspire, the virtues on which we bet our lives. Moral integrity is to adhere to this personal code of values.

Yet please remember that mistakes will be made. Our aim is to live with integrity, not obsessive perfection. It is to do our best, genuinely our best. My life story is littered with stumbles in my efforts to live up to these principles. I regret the mistakes I have made. No matter the reason or how inadvertent the error in my actions, if I know who I am and what I believe and do not act accordingly, I feel a sickening emptiness. And I hope I always will. For that pain pushes me to change and reminds me of the need for new maturity, depth, and awareness.

From my missteps I have learned and grown. In fact, I can never fully think of my mistakes as "failures" if I have learned from the experience. They were painful, difficult ways of my becoming a better person—of living with greater integrity.

The brief chapters that follow give a partial list of both values and virtues that relate most closely with a life of moral integrity. Each of these refers to our understanding of moral integrity as anchored in *a character of uncorrupted virtue,* based on *truth, fair dealing, and uprightness,* incongruent with motives based on *deception, expediency, artificiality, or shallowness.*

If you are Christian, you will feel at home with each of these. If you are not, you likely will find these values to be ones we all share—as persons of integrity, as fellow human beings wanting to live our lives to their finest and wanting successfully to live on this earth together. If you are of a religion other than Christianity, look closely at the teachings of your faith, and see if we don't hold each of these values in common.

In the midst of stumbles, I am intentional in the effort to live up to these values. It is in these that I believe and to these that I am committed. I offer them to you.

The list feels so incomplete, but at some point I had to stop. Yet it offers a foundation, a beginning. These are mine; *you* claim the values precious to *you.* And in making your own list, you don't have to stop.

CHAPTER FIVE

A LIFE OF COMPASSION

Clothe yourselves with compassion, kindness, humility,

meekness, and patience.

—Colossians 3:12

L ife can be tough. Too often there is pain, disappointment, loneliness, and loss. We say goodbye to those we love, and we are left alone. We are passed over for the position that was our heart's dream. We are told the results of an MRI by a physician in a somber tone, and then his eyes look to the floor.

Perhaps that is why the Christian faith speaks so often of compassion. There is a world in need of it. Around every corner. Across every room. Along every path.

It was midday, and my friend Billie had finished her grocery shopping with her daughters. She was checking out. The young lady bagging her groceries loved it when Billie shopped. Billie would talk with her; this young woman, who has Down syndrome, had come to know that not everyone was so gracious. As the two were finishing their business, the young woman mentioned that she was about to go on her lunch break. Billie said to her, "The girls and I are about to have lunch, too. Why don't you join us?"

Anyone who happened by Fountain Oaks Shopping Center that day would have seen the three of them, Billie and her two daughters, eating and listening attentively to the happiest luncheon guest ever invited, talking on and on—knowing she was accepted and valued and that she belonged.

I am sometimes embarrassed when I look at the same world as these remarkable people and see it with less compassion. It's as if they had been given different lenses. They see unmet needs and hungry hearts. They see opportunities to care that may blow right by me.

Some do see life differently from most of us. Artists and photographers can see beauty in what may appear a common landscape. Comedians keep us laughing over something as mundane as struggling to get pickles out of a jar. They see the world differently. Dr. Frasier Crane, the psychiatrist character on the TV show *Cheers* (and, later, on his own self-titled show), listened to one of his barstool colleagues describe an incident from his unique perspective. After a brief pause, Frasier said, "Cliff, what color is the sky in the world in which you live?"

That's it. Those with compassion see a different-color sky. They look at the world and see opportunities many of us miss, opportunities to nurture lives and touch hearts.

Love is at the heart of a life of moral integrity. I can't imagine living a life with what you and I have come to understand as integrity without *caring.* It is the epitome of *a character of uncorrupted virtue.* A life of compassion embodies the opposite of motives of *deception, expediency, artificiality, or shallowness.*

Compassion is to reach beyond myself with the simple motive of helping others. It is to care even when "I don't have a horse in that race." It is not a quid pro quo. There is no *expediency* involved. Compassion is to reach out simply because you—your welfare, your happiness, your needs—matter to me. I believe this desire is in our genetic wiring. It's on our emotional hard drive. Jesus was not telling us to begin doing it; he was reminding us that this is a part of who we already are.

Yet let's be real about this. There may be times we don't feel it. There are times we struggle with this. There may be times we have to remind ourselves to care, times when looking at the world with those lenses doesn't seem so natural.

We all have those points when we need to get back in touch with that part of our God-given selves. It's there. Maybe buried. Perhaps neglected, partially hidden. But it's there. It's the "Christ in you," as Paul wrote (Colossians 1:27). Christ abounds with grace and compassion. The Christ in each of us surely must reflect something of that likeness.

If we don't have ready access to our compassion, then we need to begin our quest to discover what is blocking us from our heartfelt caring. Does an insecurity or a defense have us living in self-serving mode? Why is "what's in it for me" our consistent default position? Is it insecurity—that we are emotionally hoarding, fearing we can't focus on another's needs because ours might not be met? Is it narcissism—a feeling of entitlement that what we want comes before all else? What is it?

If this is my struggle, then I have to discern what is blocking the God-given love I have for you, where you and your joy and welfare truly matter to me. Whatever blocks my capacity to see you through compassion's eyes, I must address.

Elizabeth Barrett Browning wrote of this concept in her poem "Aurora Leigh":

> Earth's crammed with heaven,
> And every common bush afire with God;
> But only he who sees, takes off his shoes;
> The rest sit round it and pluck blackberries.[10]

Compassion requires first that we *see*, then that we *respond*. We see the need, the opportunity to care, and we decide to seize the moment and respond.

Rarely is that response to become a missionary to Africa or to go to seminary. Sometimes. But not often. Usually it is a simple change of heart that causes us to make a difference in small ways.

Love comes in the small ways. Almost always, in the small ways. That's how compassion is usually expressed. As Mother Teresa put it, "We can do no great things; we can do small ones with great love."

To a widowed friend a loving note arrives on the anniversary date of her husband's death. It had been five years. Five years—and a friend still remembered. A small way. Easily done. Yet she sits at her breakfast table with that note in her hand and cries at being so loved. Someone remembered.

Small ways . . . that touch hearts and make a profound difference.

CHAPTER SIX

A LIFE OF TRUTH

[Love] rejoices in the truth.
—1 Corinthians 13:6

Integrity means to be true to who I am and to what I believe. To be true—to believe, to live, and to speak the truth. This idea is at the core of the definition of *moral integrity,* a life of character based on *truth.*

Earlier we focused on the harmony of integrity with our thinking, our feeling, and our action. Here we add another dimension: the congruence of what we think, feel, act, and say. In reality, of course, the spoken truth is already implied: I can't be and do the other three without saying the truth.

The word *true* has its origin in the Old English term *treo-w,* which meant loyalty and fidelity. The Germanic origin adds the concept of "faithful."[11]

Loyalty—fidelity—faithfulness. These are virtually a definition of *integrity*. As we speak, our words are in keeping with a fidelity with what we believe and who we are. When we speak, we speak with a faithfulness to the truth. To abbreviate Paul's beautiful passage to the Philippians, "Finally, beloved, whatever is true...think about these things" (4:8). Think, focus, live, and speak truthfully.

The scriptures couldn't have spoken to the issue more directly or succinctly: "Let your 'Yes' be yes and your 'No' be no" (James 5:12). Living with moral integrity—at a pretty fundamental level—means that we don't lie. The words we speak can be counted on to be the truth. This is a cornerstone both to integrity and relationships. Dishonesty destroys credibility, and the loss of credibility destroys the trust in a relationship. As children we would say to each other, "Say what you mean, and mean what you say." This basic idea of verbal integrity wasn't complex on the playground, and it isn't today. Lying may be more expedient or profitable, but it cannot be done with integrity.[12]

At about this point in any discussion on truth-telling, the question arises, "But aren't there instances when a lie can be spoken with integrity?" The answer is, of course. Such instances come along rarely, and only in a context of conflicting values, but yes.

The classic example is this: What would I do had I been hiding a Jewish family in my attic when Nazi solders came seeking their whereabouts? I'd lie in a heartbeat. And I would feel nothing but integrity. Sometimes moral values are in conflict and have to be given a pecking order. The priority of compassion in saving the lives of that family would be infinitely more important than speaking honestly to the Nazis. The greater truth here is that human life is more important than factual accuracy. The context, at times, will require discernment and decision. We have to ask ourselves: in this moment, in this context, which value is called for in bringing the greater good?

Now, we have to be careful here. Any time phrases like "the greater good" or "depending on the context" appropriately enter the conversation, there is the danger of rationalization. Ethics have to be applied to specific, real-life situations, yet applied honestly and authentically. Where values are in conflict, I cannot casually call my decision "for the greater good" when in reality I simply chose the more pleasing option.

On a lighter (but not insignificant) note, what about the

dilemma of telling the truth when it could unnecessarily hurt someone's feelings? We all have been there, in the discomforting awkwardness of that pause when a compliment may be called for that is not fully deserved. Grandma may ask, "What do you think of this dress for tonight?" referring to the print the clothing store clerk knew would one day be on the clearance rack. So what do you do? At this point you've read most of this book on integrity, so you clearly don't take truth-telling lightly. What do you say?

Again, it depends on the context, though in any context I want my words to be truthful. If she is going to embarrass herself by wearing it, I would say, "Grandma, I really think you would be more pleased at that event with something more classic and formal." If I felt the need to discourage the idea but there would be no embarrassment, I might say, "You know, that's not really my favorite." Finally, if it doesn't matter that the dress is ugly as sin, she loves it, and you want to respond with some degree of integrity, try something like, "Grandma, that dress is so you!" Integrity is maintained (and her feelings spared) by responding to the question without actually answering it. Compassion again took precedence over factual precision.

There is yet another dimension to truth-telling that can

cause much pain. I may be listening to a couple describe their arguments in marriage counseling. He may say, "Yeah, I know I'm pretty rough in the way I talk to her, and it hurts her feelings and all—but that's the way I am, and I've just got to be me." I say to him, "Well, I know just what you mean. I've got to be me, too. In fact, I've got a name for it. I call it 'integrity.' But I've discovered that for anything I may have to say to my wife, I can think of at least a dozen ways of saying it—and each of them would 'be me.' So my job is to select the one that would be spoken with the greatest respect and sensitivity to her feelings." Of course, this husband is not really dealing with integrity here—it's either laziness or simply a lack of respect for his wife's feelings.

There is a phrase in Ephesians that has always stood out to me. With a beautiful brevity, it says, "But speaking the truth in love…" (4:15). *Speak the truth in love*; there is the balance. *What* is to be spoken is the truth. *How* it is spoken is with love—with thoughtfulness, sensitivity, and respect.

A good friend is a sports analyst for college football. I was watching one of his games and saw a receiver drop an absolutely perfect pass—perfectly thrown, perfectly placed, and it would have resulted in a touchdown. As we all sometimes do, this young man had taken his eye off the ball, and, to his agony, it fell to the ground. There was a pause in the press box. I could hardly wait to hear how my friend was going to respond. How do you begin to describe such a disastrous play? He calls them as he sees them but has a way of doing it with respect for the fact that "their mamas are watching." Finally I heard his familiar voice, "Well, Joseph is not going to be pleased on Monday when he hears his coach's commentary on that one."

It has been an honor to know those who have developed the ability to be, in the same moment, both fully authentic and thoughtfully gracious.

CHAPTER SEVEN

A LIFE OF CHARACTER

Suffering produces endurance, and endurance produces character, and character produces hope, and hope does not disappoint us.
—*Romans 5:3b-5a*

Have you noticed that we don't get appalled much anymore? An author writes a moving, riveting memoir filled with accounts of things that never happened. A congressman has a freezer filled with cash. Another U.S. representative is arrested doing the very things he deemed immoral and against which he proposed legislation. An athlete mushrooms in size, big as a bull, but insists he has never knowingly used steroids.

We don't get appalled much anymore. The lack of character comes at us too often, too fast. What was appalling is now commonplace. Our senses get dulled, and we become callous, even cynical. We lose our moral sharpness.

I don't really know if there is less character these days or, because of communication technology, its absence gets more press; whichever. Our senses are being dulled. Then over time, without conscious awareness, we may lower the bar on what we expect of public figures, politicians, athletes—and even ourselves. We lose touch with the standard. English writer G. K. Chesterton said, "Art, like morality, consists in drawing the line somewhere." The line for character seems to keep moving downward. The proverbial moral compass doesn't feel so reliable.

If we expect less, we become less. We become something less than we are at our best, at our authentic best. We become something different from the person God created us to be. We lose touch with ourselves. We lose touch with our souls. We lose touch with lives of character.

I am married to a teacher. She is getting a little weary of everyone's obsession with self-esteem. "Genuine self-esteem," Karen says, "can come only when something is done to be esteemed." You can't give it away—it's got to be deserved. She'd like to see parents focus more on developing young lives of character. You see, character and integrity are the primary issues.

Once those are engaged, then self-esteem will almost inevitably follow.

Psychologist and anthropologist Mary Pipher parallels these thoughts so closely. "When we focus on self-esteem instead of character and good works, we feed into narcissism. Self-esteem, if real, is self-regard and comes from ethical behavior." She adds, "Self-esteem is probably the result, not the cause, of good work."[13]

This is confirmed by recent research. College students have been given the Narcissistic Personality Inventory for the past twenty-four years. Researchers are seeing that scores measuring self-love continue to rise across the nation in these young adults. They believe this trend is the result of the effort in our homes and schools to foster students' self-esteem. Their conclusion is that teaching students the "I am special" mantra promotes narcissism rather than self-esteem.[14] Thus teaching *self-esteem* does not achieve self-esteem, teaching *character* does.

The word *character* comes from the Greek meaning "to cut into grooves," then "to engrave."[15] Lives of character have etched into them values and principles ingrained by years of practicing what we hold to be true and worthwhile. I think of *character,* and I picture the engraver leaning over a fine piece of silver with his tools held precisely, pressing carefully into the metal. What we live, what we practice, what we ingrain becomes engraved as our character. What we live, day-to-day, we become. As Aristotle phrased it, "Moral excellence comes about as a result of habit."

In the Native American fable, the old Cherokee is teaching his grandson about life. "A fight is going on inside me. It is a terrible fight, and it is between two wolves. One is evil and the other is good. This same fight is going on inside you—and inside every other person, too."

The grandson thinks about this for a moment and asks, "In their fight, which one will win?" The old Cherokee simply replies, "The one you feed."

The values that are engraved, etched by the practice of living, become our character. The values that win are the ones we feed. Moral integrity means feeding *a character of uncorrupted virtue.*

The issue of time is implied in developing character. Time, properly used, is needed to "cut into grooves" those values. Paul was pointing to this idea in his phrase "endurance produces character" (Romans 5:4).

Practice doesn't make perfect. Practice makes permanent.

If *what* is practiced is excellent—in any realm of life—then excellence will be the likely result. If something less is practiced, then something less will result.

"Train up a child in the way he should go, and even when he is old he will not depart from it" (Proverbs 22:6 ASV). Values taught become instilled and, with time, more and more deeply engraved. It's not magic, and it's not infallible, but when young people are grounded in the character of who they are, they likely will be ready to meet life's challenges with responsibility and integrity. As noted above, in that young man or woman you will find a solid core of self-esteem reflecting a life that has earned and deserved it. You see, Paul continued in the Romans passage, "Endurance produces character, and character produces hope, and hope does not disappoint us" (Romans 5:4-5). *Character produces hope*—the hope and confidence of lives chiseled with the principles and virtues that matter.

I was amused by a quotation I read years ago attributed to Mother Teresa of Calcutta. She said, and I paraphrase here, "I know God will not give me anything I can't handle. I just wish that he didn't trust me so much." Then more recently I read with surprise her published personal letters of the decades in which she did not feel the presence or inspiration of God. I realized her earlier statement was not meant to be amusing at all.

Mother Teresa felt a call to help the poor and ill of Calcutta. It was a call that would define her life. She followed it. She lived it. Year after year those who lived in poverty were blessed because of it. Living in service was not just her way of life—it *was* her life. It became her identity, her character. Bending over beds, ladling bowls of soup, consistently engraved character into her life. She didn't wait to be inspired or to feel God's presence. She lived a life of service in the times she felt inspired, and in the times she did not. She just knew it was the right thing for her to do. She knew who she was. She had been called. She was following that call. Every morning as she awoke she followed her call. Always in character.

CHAPTER EIGHT

A LIFE OF COURAGE

"Be strong and of good courage. Do not be afraid or dismayed."
—1 Chronicles 22:13b

A few years ago when fires were raging across the dry forests of the northwestern United States, a firefighter from Colorado named David was vacationing in the state of Washington. Driving along the highway he noticed a hillside that had become engulfed in flames, with winds blowing down toward the valley.

David turned off the highway and began making his way toward the fire. As he approached it, he saw a woman trying to dig a firebreak to protect her home from the approaching fire. He later learned she was a widow living alone. All he knew then was that he had to help. David pulled in, got out of his car, and urged the woman to leave. He said to her, "You have thirty minutes, maybe less, to get your things out. Please leave now."

He then saw her seventy-seven-year-old neighbor struggling to save his house. David ran to him and said, "God as my witness, I will not let your house burn down— if you will just leave."

For the next twenty-six hours, David worked and fought. And he saved those two homes.

I heard the story on the radio, driving in to my office one morning. The interviewer was understandably awed at what David had done: for twenty-six straight hours he had fought the fire to save two strangers' homes. The interviewer was amazed—to which David simply responded, in his beautiful country accent, "Ma'am, it's what I do." When she continued gushing over his courage and commitment, he graciously interrupted her, "Ma'am, I'm a fireman. It's just what I do."

Courage is to be who we are with integrity, no matter the risk. "It's just what I do." It's just who we are.

Often those who have performed heroic acts, when interviewed, will speak with genuine humility that what they did was not heroic. It simply was the thing to do in the moment. Their courage was in remaining true to the person of compassion they were in spite of the risk. It's as Jesus said, "Perfect love casts out fear" (1 John 4:18). Perfect love—or even love that hasn't quite achieved perfection—isn't focused on oneself. The focus is on the need of another at the moment, with compassion. Courage has never meant an *absence* of fear; it is what we do, with love focused beyond ourselves, in the *presence* of fear.

Integrity means that I follow my convictions whatever the cost. When the cost is low, it is far easier to live with integrity. When risk is involved, when the cost may be high, then remaining true to those values will call for courage. As Winston Churchill put it, "Courage is rightly esteemed the first of human qualities... because it is the quality which guarantees all others."

A man I held in the highest regard during my high-school years was the father of a good friend. My buddy told me his dad once asked him, "Son, do you know what you call someone who is honest 99.9 percent of the time? Dishonest."

Living with integrity is not some obsessive-compulsive drive for perfectionism. It is a heartfelt desire *to be me,* whatever the circumstances. It is to be intentional. Even when we may be honest 99.9 percent of the time, we know that the extra 0.1 percent of the time is when the cost is higher, and courage is required.

Eighteen years into his career, a middle-aged man acknowledges to himself the only reason he has sat behind that desk for almost two decades is that it has been the family business for three generations, and he is in the family. It was expected of him, and it was safe. But it was never a passion or even a desire. It is with courage that he walks down the hallway to his father's office—and then into his new life.

A young wife once again hears her husband's profanity-laced tirade at her. It is familiar, humiliating, and abusive. She pauses, thinking of the risk. Who knows how he would respond; she could be on her own with two young children. With a deep breath and more courage than she has ever mustered, she rises to her feet and with a voice of confidence announces that she will not tolerate this behavior ever again.

Scattered across our lives are those moral moments when the word, deed, or response done with integrity may have a cost.

The price may be social, emotional, relational, or financial—but we will feel it.

Yet to do otherwise—to ignore what in our hearts we know is right—will hit harder and linger longer. I know. I've done it both ways. I've done the right thing. Other times I've chickened out. Whatever hit I may have taken in going with integrity was minor compared to the feeling of having just betrayed who I was and what I believed. Sick. I simply felt sick.

In contrast, when courage is mustered and I go with what I know is right for me—well, I don't have the word that quite describes that feeling. I know that "wholeness" isn't a feeling, but I feel *whole*. Authentic. True to who God created me to be. True to what God calls me. That feeling comes from living with integrity—and sometimes with courage.

Yet most of our lives call for another kind of courage. Few of us live in a world of genuine crises. I can't tell you the last time I saved two houses from a forest fire. For us, it's the courage needed to deal with the discomfort of losing a business deal, losing some social points by not chuckling along with an offensive joke, losing a couple of bucks by not including an improper deduction on a tax form, and the like. Most of us aren't Nelson Mandela facing decades in prison, or protesters standing in the path of tanks at Tiananmen Square.

Not us. Not often.

A less glamorous part of the definition of courage is "the ability to face difficulty or uncertainty... without being deflected from a chosen course of action." *Difficulty or uncertainty.* Not life or death. This is the courage we need in those huge blocks of time between the crises, where virtually all of life is lived.

I have known many who respond better to crisis than to day-to-day living. As someone told me on learning the subject of this book, "Often we don't know who we are until we are tested." True. It usually comes into focus in those moments. Our challenge is to remember to be that same person when there is no drama, no adrenaline, no crisis. That's where we live, and that's where our lives need the courage of day-to-day integrity.

CHAPTER NINE

A LIFE IN RELATION

*Some friends play at friendship
but a true friend sticks closer than one's nearest kin.*
—Proverbs 18:24

It was a remarkable sight. A hulking young man, easily 6' 4", had been introduced to a young boy, three years old and maybe three feet tall. The tall one folded his long legs, squatting as best he could, to shake hands.

There were few children at the reception, so Patrick took a moment to chat with young Darwin. The talk soon was of Spider-Man, and they became engaged in a most animated conversation. Other adults began looking on

*from a respectful distance at these two unlikely comrades,
but both were oblivious to any audience. Their hands were
flying through the air, drawing Spider-Man's strings from
one imagined building to another.*

*They now sat facing each other, knees to knees, eyes
locked, voices excited—enthralled in the moment. It was
just the two of them in a world of their own, along with
Spider-Man, I suppose. Little Darwin was savoring every
second of the experience, of this new friend—this giant—
joining him in his imaginary world as they leaped from
building to building to fight for freedom and justice.*

*It had been a good twenty minutes. Twenty minutes.
Can you imagine a three-year-old staying in a conversation for twenty minutes? I promise it could have gone
longer, and I can't recall why it ended. But as they were
finishing, this little three-year-old reached up, gently put
his hand on Patrick's shoulder, and said as sweetly as you
have ever heard anyone say anything, "Patrick, you do
know that Spider-Man isn't real, don't you?"*

Relationships are a gift of grace—in marriage, in family, in
friendships, with strangers. They mean the world to us. Who

hasn't resonated with Jacob's words as he was greeted by his brother, Esau: "For truly to see your face is like seeing the face of God" (Genesis 33:10).

Like seeing the face of God; we've been there. We have known those moments of precious connection. We have known times when our lives have been touched by others in ways unforeseen and undeserved. Grace. Gifts of grace.

We are built to be in relationship. As I write this, my wife, Karen, and I have just returned from the Atlanta airport. We eagerly picked up our daughter following her semester abroad in France. The wait at the airport turned out to be an interesting experience. For security reasons, everyone meeting arriving passengers waits together as one large group at the top of the escalators. Passengers for the entire airport funnel through to this one escalator and step off, only to see a few hundred expectant eyes staring at them.

It was four days before Christmas as we waited in that excited crowd. If you ever question the importance of relationships, go to the airport and stand with that group just before Christmas. Scattered among us were "Welcome Home!" signs, balloons, Santa hats, and one fellow wearing reindeer antlers. Often you would hear a scream from the crowd, and someone would run down the corridor for a long-anticipated, tearful embrace.

A woman to our left was straining for a glimpse of her son, daughter-in-law, and four grandchildren, "all between the ages of seven and seven months," who live in France. The woman to our right was waiting for her son from Seattle. She was often on the phone with her husband as she learned updates on the flight arrival. Her voice defined anticipation. "We haven't seen him since February," she told me, her eyes immediately brimming with tears. "I'm so sorry," she said, apologizing for her emotion. "He's in the Navy and has to fly back Christmas Day for Iraq." She stopped me as I began to express my regret at such a short stay. "No," she said, "we feel blessed to have the time and are going to savor every minute."

We are built to be in relationship. We each connect in our unique ways with different personalities and relational styles, but we share in common that need for connection. We need closeness. We need to be accepted and understood. Remember when a friend cared and listened to you talk about a hurt inflicted on you? You began to feel the healing of that wound. Something began to change just in speaking of it aloud in the loving presence of another.

Like seeing the face of God.

Or you may have received a phone call on a day that was special for you. Your graduation day. The first morning on your new job. The appointment at which you would get the report from the fertility specialist. The day you were moving your mom into Hospice. As you were about to leave the house, the phone rang. It was your friend. She would be thinking of you. And, oh— she'd be home later, if you felt like calling.

Like seeing the face of *God*.

We are built to be in community. For decades our family has hung out with friends with whom we surely will grow old. We cannot imagine their not being in our lives. They are our dear friends. With us in the good times, for us in the struggles. Together we have fought cancer, worried about children, buried loved ones, played golf, and laughed until we cried.

We are built to be in community. Our lives are completed by relationships. Of course, we can't depend on anyone outside of ourselves to provide the core of purpose, meaning, and joy. That has to come from within. Those we love don't create it, but they certainly do complete it. Relationships, especially marriage, are the icing on the cake. Again, it's not the cake itself. I have to bring all the ingredients myself for the core happiness. But, my, how that icing tops it off!

Jesus highlighted the importance of relationships in an

interesting way: "For where two or three are gathered in my name, I am there among them" (Matthew 18:20). We know what he means. We have been there. There is a spiritual quality present as we gather with those who matter the most to us.

It is a lot like seeing the face of God.

Yet sacred moments—as with Patrick and Darwin—are often not limited to connecting with the tried and true. If we are open, there are chance moments with those we will know only in precious passing. How many times do I remind myself of Elizabeth Barrett Browning's exquisite lines using Moses as her metaphor: "Earth's crammed with heaven, / And every common bush afire with God: / But only he who sees, takes off his shoes" ("Aurora Leigh"). Only those who are open to the experience of God by being fully human and available to relationship will know how beautiful the moment really is.

Meaningful relationships. Lasting or in passing. For a lifetime or for a season. They are precious, even sacred. I think of the lines from the finale of the musical *Les Misérables*:

> And remember the truth that once was spoken,
> To love another person is to see the face of God.[16]

CHAPTER TEN

A LIFE OF FIDELITY

Many proclaim themselves loyal,
but who can find one worthy of trust?
The righteous walk in integrity.
—Proverbs 20:6-7a

I sit with a couple. She is doubled over in pain. Last week she learned of his affair. It had gone on for almost a year. She slowly tells me first of the devastation she has felt in the past few days. Then he begins to tell the story.

"We're just so different," he explained. They had different personalities, different interests, and began going in different directions. They became less and less connected. Each knew it, but neither really made an issue of it. No

one said, "I don't know you anymore and haven't felt married in years. We've got to get some help. We can't continue this way."

Instead, they made their peace with being married to spouses they didn't know. Married—yet each desperately lonely. But neither blowing the whistle. Neither calling the question. She complained about the garbage still sitting there, and he about her running late—but not a word was spoken of the miles that had come to separate them.

Then he met a new female colleague at work. They were together on a project. Sometimes they would grab a quick lunch. Sometimes they had to work late to meet a deadline. "We began as friends," he said. "Finally I had someone with whom I could be myself. We had so much in common. It's like we could finish each other's sentences. It just got out of hand."

Loneliness was a terrible thing for both spouses. Each had contributed to their getting there, truth be known, about equally. Neither had done a bloomin' thing to work on it—again about equally. That was their first moral decision—they made it passively together—to decide not to really work on their marriage. Assuming at some level they wanted to be married—and their sitting in my office points to that likelihood—then this decision for inaction was their first breach of fidelity.

Without a word, a white towel was silently thrown into the ring.

Then he met his new colleague.

Affairs are powerful. Whenever I hear how one began, I consistently have the image of someone creeping closer and closer to look over the edge of the top of a waterfall. With the beginning of this friendship there is the curiosity, the connection, then the rush of emotion—all encouraging them closer and closer to the edge. Then one step too many is taken toward the edge of that slope.

When the friendship becomes romantic, infatuation kicks in. This infatuation makes moral decision-making more difficult. This is where rationalizing can make a tragic joke of anything resembling integrity.

"I didn't feel appreciated...or understood...or heard..." Finish the sentence any way you like, but that tends to be how it goes. The affair begins. Fidelity is lost.

There is an effective way to avoid getting close to the edge of the waterfall in any relationship that challenges fidelity: Watch for the line toward infidelity. Avoid the first step across it. How? By asking a simple question: *Would I say or do what I am about to say or do with this person if my spouse were sitting here with us?* If so, then it is probably not a step toward infidelity. If not, it probably is.

Fidelity comes in many forms. Marital fidelity is the one that gets the most press because it is the most painful when it is violated. There is fidelity to principles, to values, to agreements, to covenants, to the good faith of promises made. *Fidelity* means "loyalty to an allegiance, promise, or vow." *Any significant allegiance, promise, or vow.* Remember that moral integrity is incongruent with *deception, expediency, artificiality, or shallowness.* Infidelity involves all of them.

Fidelity implies that we will be loyal and can be trusted. Our word is our bond. We will follow through on what we promised. We can be counted on; trusted. Sounds like lessons we learned in scouting—basic and important.

CHAPTER ELEVEN

A LIFE OF RESPECT

Pay to all what is due them . . . respect to whom respect is due,
honor to whom honor is due.
—Romans 13:7

Robert Coles, the Harvard psychiatrist known for his work with children of poverty and crisis, recalls one moment in his life that had as profound an effect as any he ever had experienced. He was to meet with Dorothy Day, known internationally in the Catholic Church for her work with those who are homeless.

On the day of their meeting, Dr. Coles went into the room and saw Ms. Day sitting with a homeless woman,

patiently listening to her. The woman was drunk, but Ms.
Day sat listening to her, nodding and occasionally asking
a question. Dr. Coles stood there respectfully. Finally, Ms.
Day saw him and graciously asked the woman if she could
interrupt her for a moment. She turned to Dr. Coles and
asked—and here is the moment that touched him so
deeply: "Are you waiting to talk with one of us?"[17]
(emphasis added)

Respect. Profound, personal respect.

This woman of international reputation so respected the
woman with whom she sat that she did not assume for a moment
it was she for whom Dr. Coles was waiting. It was an intuitive,
spontaneous response—the kind that comes straight from the
heart. What would most of us have said? "I'll be with you in just
a minute."

Respect is to relate with dignity and consideration. Respect
involves what psychologist Carl Rogers called in his writings
"unconditional positive regard."[18] It is an attitude of acceptance
and understanding.

I remember years ago, a homeless woman stayed for several
months somewhere near our church. We would see her periodi-

cally as she would slip in to freshen up in one of our restrooms. She was a private person, especially because she did not know if she was welcome. When we saw her, we would speak and greet her by name. One day, not long before she left, she stopped and engaged one of our staff in a rare conversation. She just wanted to say "thank you"—thank you for speaking kindly, and especially for calling her by her name.

An attitude of respect toward others implies much about our attitude toward ourselves. Respect points to humility. The word *humility* comes from the Latin *humus,* meaning "earth." Those who walk with humility are grounded. Humility does indeed mean that we don't think too highly of ourselves. But it also means we are grounded in who we genuinely are. It means we are grounded in the values and principles we believe and by which our lives are defined. The humble stand side by side as sisters and brothers together. As peers. No one better than anyone else. Respect. Mutual respect.

Racism, sexism, elitism of any kind has its foundation in an absence of respect. The world has a way of diminishing those who are perceived as different from the majority. Often they are given a name as a way of making them as something less. The rural become "rednecks," the homeless "bums," and every racial and ethnic group has its barbed slang aimed at it. This lack of respect, this dehumanizing, springs from insecurity. If I am not grounded in who I am, then I feel anxious and insecure. Since I don't feel worthy, I must diminish you. I must make you lesser so I don't feel quite so bad about myself. Or I must go with the cultural majority to feel the illusion of security. Arrogance is founded in the same insecurity. It is the opposite of self-confidence. Arrogance is a smokescreen. It's bluster, a façade that wants to look big because of feeling so small. It's overcompensation out of that insecurity. Those who are self-confident have no need to inflate themselves or diminish others.

We are all aware of a lessening of respect seen in the past couple of decades, especially in politics. It is as though, *If I am right, then you have to be wrong.* Talk radio is filled with both sides calling each other idiots because they look at an issue differently. The polarizing effect is profound. The disrespect is absolute. *If I am right, then you are wrong. If my side is right and yours is wrong, then we have nothing to discuss until you see the fallacy of your thinking, concede, and agree with me.* The competitiveness and the rigidity abort any meaningful, mutual search for the truth. This arrogance does not allow one side to see the value and validity in the points the other is making. Those who disagree are not only wrong, they are idiots. The disrespect is profound.

I can respect a perspective and disagree with it at the same time. Countless times I have been in discussions with persons I respect but with whom I disagree. Obviously there are perspectives that I *don't* respect, like those of terrorists or racists. I do not see them as remotely valid, because of their clear lack of moral integrity and the absence of core values. But that is the exception.

Most of these polarizing conversations in our society are between those who share broad, common values but differ in how they should be applied.

No reasonable person would want a human being to be hungry, but reasonable persons may differ on the solutions as to how our nation best addresses poverty. I do not respect a point of view that has no compassion, but I do respect the truth in a variety of perspectives that differ on how compassion should be enacted. And if we find ourselves in genuine conversation instead of polarized as adversaries, we may gain value from perspectives with which we do not ultimately agree. We all may be enriched by having moved out of our rigid, narrow worlds and viewing life from another vantage point.

We need one another. None of us has a corner on the truth. This communication requires openness, which takes respect.

Remember the Amish response to the tragedy of October 2006? It was such a contrast in this time of polarization. In the hamlet of Nickel Mines, Pennsylvania, a man tied ten Amish schoolgirls together and shot them, killing five. He then killed himself. The Amish response as a people of faith was consistent. I watched as their representative publicly thanked the nation for the many contributions that had been sent in. He said they would be used for medical expenses of the children injured. Then he added that, of course, part of the money would go toward counseling for the family of the man who had done this, since this was an incredibly difficult time for them.

That same day, about seventy-five people attended the man's funeral. Over half of them were Amish.

Respect for all. For all of God's children. Respect for all *as* God's children.

CHAPTER TWELVE

REMEMBERING

And do you not remember?
—Mark 8:18

You've got to love the Pharisees. Bless their devious little hearts! They were always trying to trip Jesus up with their questions. But his answers to them have given us some of his richest teachings.

One of them asked him, "Teacher, which commandment in the law is the greatest?" You could just see the crowd leaning in. Jesus answered, " 'You shall love the Lord your God with all your heart, and with all your soul, and with all your mind.' "

The crowd relaxed. In fact, they began nodding. It was exactly what they expected him to say. It was straight out of the book of Deuteronomy.

Jesus went on, "This is the greatest and first commandment." And the nodding continued. "And a second is like it...."

The nodding stopped. What second is like it? What second is there to be like it?

Jesus continued, "'You shall love your neighbor as yourself'" (Matthew 22:34-39).

How do you love the Lord your God? How do you give traction to your love? How do you give it meaning in life? By loving your neighbor as yourself.

I believe that. I love the Lord my God, and I *want* to love my neighbor as I love myself. I do. I really do.

But, you know—life keeps coming at me really fast. *You* know, the calendar, the obligations... I really would like to find the time to love my neighbor—but, you know...

Yes, you *do* know. And you know what my problem is. It's not really that I get too busy; *I get too self-absorbed.* By the time I finish "loving self," I run out of time and steam and focus on loving neighbor.

I forget what else is important.

Several years ago I got a number enabling me to run in the New York Marathon. I was psyched! I trained for

months to get ready. Then the weekend before the big
event, at the eleven-mile mark of a twelve-mile run, something gave way in my right leg. I limped home.

I was obsessed with the leg all week. Would it heal in
time? Would I get to run? Now, make no mistake, Karen
Greer was going to New York whether I ran the thing or
not! But I so wanted to run. I was testing the leg, stretch-
ing it all week. Embarrassingly obsessed.

As we flew up, I was checking my leg. We went to a
matinee that afternoon, but I wasn't paying much attention. It was about some guy with half a mask or something.
I was obsessed with the leg.

The marathon began on Staten Island. To get there
we caught the buses about 6:00 A.M. in front of the New
York Public Library. I remember standing there in line, of
course, checking my leg. How was it feeling? Was it going
to last?

The line moved up toward the buses. Just as I was
about to board, another volunteer came up to the one helping us and pointed to an elderly, blind couple standing a
few feet away. He explained that each morning at 6:00
they caught their bus in front of the library to get to work.

With all of the marathon buses in the way, they didn't know where to catch their bus. They were nervous about getting to their jobs and confused as to what to do.

I looked at them. There stood an elderly, blind couple. They were terribly confused and frightened.

And I had been worried about my leg. . . . How embarrassing.

I had become so self-absorbed, so consumed with me, that I had lost all sight of perspective, of what really matters in life. I had lost touch with the values that ground me. I felt lousy.

About that time someone yelled at me, "Move along up there!" As I stood there staring, I had been holding up the line. I moved along and got on the bus.

Wearing my running shorts, I didn't have a dime on me to give them for cab fare. All I could do was watch them as my bus pulled away and promise myself I always would remember . . .

> *Remember what truly matters in life,*
> *and what is of far less importance . . .*
> *Remember my integrity,*
> *remember the values at my center,*

the values that define me.

I promised myself at that moment I would never for-
get. Never.

And, of course, I do.

I forget. Fortunately, not honesty or fidelity; those are pretty set. It's the compassion, and at times the humility and respect.
I get distracted and instinctively go back to one of my old default
settings. I forget.

The word *remember* comes from the Latin for "memory." It
is to call back the memory. It is to reconnect, to recall, to reclaim
a memory of value that has been lost.

How will you do that? How will you consistently remember
those values that define your integrity? Find your images to help
you maintain that focus. Find your metaphors for the values you
most easily lose. Find your image, your memory that will help
you recall and reconnect with who you truly are. When I lose
touch with my compassion and humility, my metaphor will
always be that blind, elderly couple standing with their canes in
the dark, needing help in getting through life.

I see their faces. And I remember.

EPILOGUE

The cross is such a powerful symbol. It is an image that stays with us as Christians. It's never far away. It stands in the front of our sanctuaries and at the center of our faith. It connects us with the heart of the story.

To persons of faith the cross stands for so much. One of its meanings for me is as a symbol of integrity.

> *He didn't want to do it. He even asked if it would be possible for that cup to pass him by. He didn't have to do it. He could have hidden or simply gone another way. He could have been more discreet—holding back here or there so as not to offend—and the whole ugly episode would never have happened.*

That was not Jesus. Whatever the circumstances, he would be Jesus. He was true to the spirit of I Am Who I Am. He lived with integrity.

There are days when I sit in the quiet of the sanctuary. It is a moment of meditation. I am not much aware of what is around me. My eyes are open, but I am not taking it in.

Then I look up, and there is the cross—a beautiful bronze cross set in white marble. At the center of the cross, where the two timbers meet, is a bronze circle. It is a halo, for the Christ. This circle represents his holiness, to be sure. But every time I see it—this complete circle—I also think of his *wholeness*. In every moment of his life he was true to who he was. Whole, congruent, perfectly authentic.

He lived in the midst of a lonely and isolated world. He had to get his message out no matter who it upset. He would let nothing intimidate or dissuade him from proclaiming the undying love of Almighty God.

He spoke to a world that needed to hear. He spoke of love, and in so doing, he gave all that he had. He loved us to death.

Anything less would have had no integrity. Anything less would be less than he was.

In the quiet of the sanctuary I look up, and I am reminded to be all I was created to be.

NOTES

Prologue

1. Eric Partridge, *Origins: A Short Etymological Dictionary of Modern English* (New York: Macmillan, 1966), p. 468. I am grateful to Donald Davis, from whom I first learned of the origin of the word *parable*.

Part I. Personal Integrity: A Life of Wholeness

1. *The American Heritage Dictionary of the English Language,* Fourth Edition (Boston: Houghton Mifflin Company, 2000), p. 910.

2. *Chambers Dictionary of Etymology,* Robert K. Barnhart, ed. (Edinburgh: Chambers Harrap Publishers, 1988), p. 535.

3. Stephen L. Carter, *Integrity* (New York: HarperCollins, 1996), p. 18.

4. Patrick Thomas Malone and Thomas Patrick Malone, *The Windows of Experience: Moving Beyond Recovery to Wholeness* (New York: Simon & Schuster, 1992), pp. 154, 161.

5. Eric Partridge, *Origins: A Short Etymological Dictionary of Modern English,* p. 301. I am appreciative to Bert Gary, from whom I learned of this distinction in his book *Jesus Unplugged*.

6. Parker J. Palmer, *Let Your Life Speak: Listening for the Voice of Vocation* (San Francisco: Jossey-Bass, 2000), p. 3.

7. Partridge, *Origins: A Short Etymological Dictionary of Modern English*, p. 33.

8. Lynne McFall, "Integrity" in *Ethics and Personality,* John Deigh, ed. (Chicago: The University of Chicago Press, 1992), p. 80.

9. Carter, *Integrity,* p. 7.

10. From an address by Elie Wiesel at Emory University on January 18, 1983.

11. *Merriam-Webster's Collegiate Dictionary,* Eleventh Edition (Springfield, Mass.: Merriam-Webster, 2005), p. 1032.

12. This quotation, though said with humor, points to what is referred to as the "attribution error." It is the tendency we have to focus on another's personality (and character shortcomings) when explaining their behavior, but on our circumstances when explaining our own. The danger of being judgmental toward others' actions and rationalizing for our own is obvious.

13. Thomas Jefferson, *Notes on the State of Virginia* (New York: Penguin Putnam, 1999), p. 169.

14. Sheldon Kopp, *Who Am I...Really? An Autobiographical Exploration on Becoming Who You Are* (New York: Macmillan, 1987), p. 4.

15. Ibid., p. 68.

16. Thomas Keating, *The Heart of the World: A Spiritual Catechism* (New York: Crossroad Publishing Co., 1981), p. 69.

17. Michael Bamberger and Don Yaeger, "Over the Edge: Aware

That Drug Testing Is a Sham, Athletes Seem to Rely More Than Ever on Banned Performance Enhancers," *Sports Illustrated,* April 14, 1997.

18. National Public Radio Day to Day, " 'Integrity' Most Looked-Up Word in Online Dictionary," December 27, 2005.

19. Suzanne Braun Levine, *Inventing the Rest of Our Lives: Women in Second Adulthood* (New York: Penguin, 2005), p. 57.

20. William Bridges, *Transitions: Making Sense of Life's Changes* (New York: Da Capo Press, 2004), p. 133.

21. Thomas Merton, *A Search for Solitude: Pursuing the Monk's True Life* (San Francisco: HarperSanFrancisco, 1996), p. 159.

22. Elaine Pagels, *Beyond Belief: The Secret Gospel of Thomas* (New York: Vintage Books, 2003), p. 32.

23. In Barbara Brown Taylor, *Leaving Church: A Memoir of Faith* (San Francisco: HarperSanFrancisco, 2006), p. 7.

24. Jim Wallis, *God's Politics: Why the Right Gets It Wrong and the Left Doesn't Get It* (San Francisco: HarperSanFrancisco, 2005), p. xiv.

25. Bridges, *Transitions,* pp. xii, 129.

26. George Leonard and Michael Murphy, *The Life We Are Given: A Long-Term Program for Realizing the Potential of Body, Mind, Heart, and Soul* (New York: Tarcher/Penguin, 1995), p. 47.

27. Gail Godwin, *The Finishing School* (New York: Viking Penguin, 1984), p. 4.

Part II. Moral Integrity: A Person of Values

1. *The Oxford English Dictionary,* Second Edition (Oxford: Clarendon Press, 1989), p. 1066.

2. *Webster's Third New International Dictionary of the English Language Unabridged* (Springfield, Mass.: Merriam-Webster, 1986), p. 1174.

3. Louis P. Pojman, *Ethics: Discovering Right and Wrong,* Fifth Edition (Belmont, Calif.: Thomson Wadsworth, 2006), p. 27.

4. Ibid., p. 70.

5. Palmer, *Let Your Life Speak: Listening for the Voice of Vocation,* p. 3.

6. Partridge, *Origins: A Short Etymological Dictionary of Modern English,* p. 760.

7. Lawrence Kohlberg, *Child Psychology and Childhood Education: A Cognitive-Developmental View* (New York: Longman, 1987), p. 283.

8. J. K. Rowling, *Harry Potter and the Chamber of Secrets* (New York: Scholastic, 1999), p. 333.

9. Mark Frost, *The Grand Slam: Bobby Jones, America, and the Story of Golf* (New York: Hyperion, 2004), pp. 227-28.

10. Elizabeth Barrett Browning, *Aurora Leigh,* Norton Critical Edition (New York: W. W. Norton & Co., 1996), p. 238.

11. Partridge, *Origins: A Short Etymological Dictionary of Modern English,* p. 740.

12. There is an interesting distinction to note here. When what is spoken is not lived, it is indeed a violation of integrity—but, technically, not necessarily a result of lying. It may be the result of weakness or hypocrisy. If the person meant it when he said it, then the violation of his action was out of weakness. If he did not mean it when he spoke it—indeed, he lied—then it was out of his hypocrisy. Whether the words were believed when they were spoken makes the difference. For

example, when an alcoholic says sincerely that drunkenness is wrong, it is from the weakness of his addiction that he periodically may give in to the temptation. He told the truth. But he didn't act on it. He is not living up to what he believes. Though he is not lying, he is not living with integrity—where his (spoken) thoughts, feelings, and actions are in sync. Yet if an athlete publicly states that taking anabolic steroids is wrong while he is using them, then his breach of integrity is hypocrisy. He is lying. It's not that he isn't living up to what he believes—he doesn't believe what he says. I am grateful to ethicist John Truslow for this distinction.

13. Mary Pipher, *The Shelter of Each Other* (New York: Grosset/Putnam, 1996), p. 158.

14. *Wilson Quarterly,* Autumn 2008, p. 14.

15. Partridge, *Origins: A Short Etymological Dictionary of Modern English,* p. 92.

16. From *Les Misérables,* the musical, book by Claude-Michel Schönberg and Alain Boublil, lyrics by Herbert Kretzmer and Alain Boublil, based upon the 1862 novel by Victor Hugo.

17. Robert Coles, *Dorothy Day: A Radical Devotion* (New York: Da Capo Press, 1987), p. xvii.

18. Carl R. Rogers and Barry Stevens, *Person to Person: The Problem of Being Human—A New Trend in Psychology* (Lafayette, Calif.: Real People Press, 1967), p. 54.

REFLECTION / DISCUSSION GUIDE

Written by Sally D. Sharpe

The following questions may be used in a time of personal reflection or group discussion. More questions are provided than you may have time to discuss in a group session. They are here to give you ideas and options. Read through the questions in advance and note those you would like your group to discuss, or ask group members to select the questions that speak to them. For any given chapter, feel free to begin the discussion simply by asking your group what was meaningful or what resonated with them.

For group discussion, here are three alternatives for how to group the discussion questions, based on the number of sessions you want to devote to the ideas from this book. (You may find that the material will lend itself best to four sessions, though any of these options is workable, depending on your time.)

For two sessions, group the questions as follows:
Session 1: Part I, chapters 1–4
Session 2: Part II, chapters 5–12

For four sessions, group the questions as follows:

Session 1: Part I, chapters 1 and 2

Session 2: chapters 3 and 4

Session 3: Part II, chapters 5–7

Session 4: chapters 8–12

For six sessions, group the questions as follows:

Session 1: Part I, chapter 1

Session 2: chapters 2 and 3

Session 3: chapter 4

Session 4: Part II, Introduction

Session 5: chapters 5–7

Session 6: chapters 8–12

PART I. PERSONAL INTEGRITY: A LIFE OF WHOLENESS

1. Does the following statement of Hendrik Kraemer help you in remaining anchored in life: "If you know who you are, you will know what to do"? If so, how?

2. What does *integrity* mean to you? How does your thinking match with the author's two understandings of integrity?

Chapter 1. Markers of Integrity

1. How is integrity much more than doing the right thing and telling the truth?

2. What does "engage in our own discernment" mean to you? How can this lead us to integrity or wholeness? How have you gone about doing this?

3. Read Luke 15:11-32. Does the parable of the prodigal son resonate with you as a journey to integrity?

4. Have you ever felt you were on the wrong track with your life, that you were not living the life for which you were created? How were you aware of it? What did you do?

5. Do you agree with the author that the appropriate question in faithful living is not "Does it feel good?" but rather "Does it feel right?" Why or why not?

6. What does it mean to "live life in the gray"? Why is this often so difficult?

7. Read Matthew 19:16-22. What was this man's struggle? Can you identify with it?

8. Recall a time when clarity, commitment, and courage enabled you to live with integrity and be true to who you are. What did you do? How did it feel?

Chapter 2. Wandering Off Your Path

1. Why do you think we often find ourselves in the middle of our lives without integrity? What happens? Why do we so regularly wander off the path?

2. What happens when we ignore integrity and no longer make moral and ethical values a priority in decision-making? How does it feel?

3. When have you found yourself living in the tension between conflicting attitudes, desires, or beliefs? What happened? How did you decide what to do?

4. What does it mean to say that selfishness without honesty is at the heart of rationalization?

5. What happens when the lines are blurred between our social self and our authentic self—between what the world expects of us and the persons God created us to be? How important is it to distinguish between the two? Explain your answer.

6. Why do so many of us become disconnected from our true selves in childhood? How does the family play a part in this process? How can family foster authenticity?

7. Respond to the following statement: parenting isn't shaping our children nearly so much as helping them discover what shape their lives already have been given.

8. Why will taking a path that is "not your own" never work?

Chapter 3. Three Detours

1. It has been said that "sin is when we think we are less than we are or greater than we are or anything other than who we are." Is it difficult for you to think of sin in these terms? Why or why not?

2. How is self-esteem related to this idea of living with integrity?

3. How can the pressure to perform and "measure up" lead to struggles with self-esteem?

4. What is your understanding of narcissism? Have you ever felt narcissistic? With what had you lost touch? How did it distance you from your true self?

5. How would you describe "greatness with integrity"?

6. In your own words, how would you explain the concept of "drifting"? When we have drifted, what questions can help us get back on track?

7. What is involved for you in the search for integrity? What can help you discover who you are?

8. What does it mean to "stay awake" in the context of integrity? How realistic is it?

Chapter 4. Who Am I Now?

1. Is there such a thing as an "old beginning"? Is a life of old beginnings a life with marginal integrity? Have you ever been there?

2. How important is it for us to stay current with what our life purpose is now, today?

3. How do you best go about *discerning anew* who you are now and where you are going? How have you kept in touch with that as a process?

4. How do life transitions begin? What are the common elements in that passage? What has been your personal experience of this?

5. What have your "times of reflection" been like?

6. Would you agree that many of life's most important decisions are not made but discovered? Why or why not?

7. Are endings necessary to new beginnings? Explain your answer.

8. Why do you think we tend to resist change? What holds us back? What happens when we try to live in the past?

PART II. MORAL INTEGRITY: A PERSON OF VALUES

1. Are both *personal integrity* and *moral integrity* critical to a proper understanding of integrity? Why or why not?

2. Is it possible that Adolph Hitler does pass the first "test" of integrity, though not the second? Explain your answer.

3. Considering the two "starting points" from which we arrive at our moral base, how has each been important to you?

4. How do the traditional seven virtues match with what you think of as the core values of the Christian faith?

5. How important is it to aspire to level III of Lawrence Kohlberg's levels of moral development? How realistic is it?

6. How can we discover our genuine values? How does knowing our values help us meet the challenges of life?

7. By which values is your life defined?

Chapter 5. A Life of Compassion

1. What is involved in a life of compassion?

2. How does the idea of the "Christ in you" (from Colossians 1:27) relate to compassion?

3. What are the common obstacles that can block heartfelt compassion? With which of these obstacles do you struggle most often?

4. Respond to Mother Teresa's quotation: "We can do no great things; we can do small ones with great love." How does this resonate with you? What are some of the "small ones" that have touched you most deeply?

Chapter 6. A Life of Truth

1. After reading this chapter, what does living a life of truth mean to you?

2. Must a life of integrity be based on truth? Why or why not?

3. Is it ever possible for a lie to be spoken with integrity? Why or why not? How does consideration for the greater good come into play?

4. How have you handled those dilemmas of telling the truth when it could unnecessarily hurt someone's feelings?

5. Who have been your mentors in being both fully authentic and thoughtfully gracious?

Chapter 7. A Life of Character

1. What does it mean to you to live a life of character?

2. Have we have lowered our expectations regarding character in recent years? If so, why do you think this has happened?

3. Respond to this statement: "If we expect less, we become less."

4. Would you agree that focusing on self-esteem, rather than character, leads to narcissism? Why or why not? Do you believe that self-esteem is the *result* rather than the cause of character? Why or why not?

5. When you think of character, who comes to mind? Briefly describe that person or those persons.

Chapter 8. A Life of Courage

1. What does *courage* mean to you?

2. Does courage differ from being fearless? Explain your answer.

3. Why is courage sometimes required when remaining true to our values?

4. It has been said that often we do not know who we are until we are tested. Have you experienced that in your life? If so, in what ways?

5. What does it mean to exhibit the courage of "day-to-day integrity"?

Chapter 9. A Life in Relation

1. In what ways are relationships a gift of grace?

2. Do you resonate with the idea that connecting with a caring friend is like "seeing the face of God"? If so, how? Do you remember a specific moment that brought this idea to mind?

3. What does it mean to say that our lives are "completed" by relationships? When have you found a sense of completeness in community?

4. Have you ever shared a sacred moment with a total stranger? What happened? What can help us be open to experiencing God in moments such as this?

Chapter 10. A Life of Fidelity

1. After reading this chapter, how would you describe *fidelity*? What does fidelity imply?

2. Review the waterfall analogy in this chapter. How do we most effectively avoid getting close to the edge of the waterfall in any relationship that challenges fidelity?

3. Besides marital fidelity, what are other allegiances, promises, or agreements deserving of our fidelity?

4. What can help us cultivate loyalty and faithfulness in our lives?

Chapter 11. A Life of Respect

1. How would you describe *respect*?

2. Psychologist Carl Rogers says that respect involves "unconditional positive regard." What does this mean?

3. What does an attitude of respect toward others imply about our attitude toward ourselves?

4. Do you think we have seen a lessening of respect, especially in politics? Why or why not?

5. Do you believe it is possible to respect a perspective and also disagree with it at the same time? Why or why not?

6. How are we enriched by viewing life from another vantage point?

Chapter 12. Remembering

1. If busyness is the *excuse* we give for not loving our neighbors as we should, what is the underlying *reason* we fail to do so?

2. What causes us to become self-absorbed and to forget what is truly important in life? Have you had those times in your life?

3. Based on the origin of the word *remembering,* what does the term mean to you? Why is it so important to remember—to reconnect and reclaim—the values that define one's integrity?

4. How will you consistently remember those values which define *your* integrity? Is there an image, a memory, that will bring you back to who you are at your finest and most authentic?

Also by Ronald J. Greer

ISBN 978-1-4267-4191-3

We don't stop being parents when our kids are grown, but some things do change. *Now That They Are Grown* aims to help readers avoid as many potholes as possible in making the transition from parenting children to being parents of young adults. Here are ways to nurture our adult children while encouraging their independence and maturity. It is a new day in our relationship with our children. The page has been turned, and we are now writing the new chapter in the life of our family. It is important that we get it right.

"Ron is a wise and helpful guide for parents looking for mature, healthy relationships with their adult children. Ron's words not only educate, but they also encourage parents that they can do this! *Now That They Are Grown* is a job well done!" —**Dr. Bill Britt, senior minister, Peachtree Road United Methodist Church**

ISBN 978-0-687-33363-9

Also, regarding Markings on the Windowsill:

"By transforming a terrible tragedy into a time of deepening faith, Ron shows the rest of us the way." —**William H. Willimon, author and United Methodist bishop**

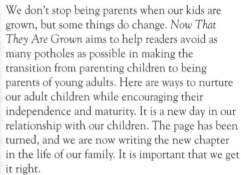 **Abingdon Press**

CPSIA information can be obtained
at www.ICGtesting.com
Printed in the USA
LVHW020233240819
628657LV00010B/110

9 781501 898716